T0246339

TAKE MY NAME BUT SAY IT SLOW

Take My Name
but Say It Slow

ESSAYS

THOMAS DAI

W. W. NORTON & COMPANY

Independent Publishers Since 1923

Take My Name but Say It Slow is a work of nonfiction. Certain names have been changed.

Photograph on p. 14 by Sheng Dai. Photograph on p. 54 by Ailing Wang. Photograph on p. 170 by Daniel Xu. All other photographs by the author.

For information about permission to reproduce selections from this book, write to Permissions, W. W. Norton & Company, Inc., 500 Fifth Avenue, New York, NY 10110

For information about special discounts for bulk purchases, please contact W. W. Norton Special Sales at specialsales@wwnorton.com or 800-233-4830

Manufacturing by Lakeside Book Company
Book design by Daniel Lagin
Production manager: Louise Mattarelliano

ISBN 978-1-324-06637-8

W. W. Norton & Company, Inc., 500 Fifth Avenue, New York, NY 10110
www.wwnorton.com

W. W. Norton & Company Ltd., 15 Carlisle Street, London W1D 3BS

10 9 8 7 6 5 4 3 2 1

It begins in delight, it inclines to the impulse, it assumes direction with the first line laid down, it runs a course of lucky events, and ends in a clarification of life—not necessarily a great clarification, such as sects and cults are founded on, but in a momentary stay against confusion.

—ROBERT FROST, "THE FIGURE A POEM MAKES"

I was a shape but one where everything inside me was in motion and I was trying to hold it mathematically, trying to be a pattern in the world.

—RENEE GLADMAN, *CALAMITIES*

Contents

TAKE MY NAME BUT SAY IT SLOW

Map Page

I am trying to envision a map. It is maybe the map of my life.

On it are the usual features by which a person can be placed: a hometown in a valley with mountains to its east. A bend in the river, a road. There are cities in the distance, most of them indistinct. One is surrounded by desert; another hangs suspended over an alluvial plain. Details begin coalescing in and around these sites. Empty rooms leading to other enclosures, a house on a hill, a bridge covered in hieroglyphs, a pond whose surface never stirs, a red cliffside, a field. Two continents dominate the map, two landmasses that, by traveling between them, the mapmaker has caused to draw near.

I want to see the map first, and then write it: write it fast, write it true. As if one could capture the thing as it happens, an instantaneous outline of experience. As if one could fix it, fix the self, and in that locating create a spatially sensible life.

When I give up on seeing this map, it will be a different kind of finding—I will no longer wish to be framed.

EVERY MAP TELLS A STORY. THE STORY A MAP TENDS TO TELL IS *this is here* and *that is there* and all these placements are real and scientific and natural—a story of the world as knowable, as set. Maps are only as impartial as their makers, though, and most makers have "world views" to impart. It was only in the sixteenth and seventeenth centuries—the so-called "Age of Discovery," a time when Europeans became invested in showing who owned what and where and whom—that maps as we know them began to proliferate. (Prior to this period, cartography had been an outré pastime, and most maps resembled the primitive diagrams housed in people's brains as opposed to accurate renderings of space helpful for world exploration and conquest.) Early maps represented the interests of the states that produced and disseminated them, authorizing one subjective world view as true. Both then and now, cartographers conditioned their maps to lie flat and deceptively silent, camouflaging their claims as boring, indubitable facts.

Not every map displays such faith, or hubris, in objectivity. We all generate our own cartographies—spatial images documenting lost places, hidden byways, who we were at that time, that place. Growing up, I loved looking at maps for precisely this reason: the license they gave me to imagine the world differently, to put it in order in my own, slapdash way. The first map I can remember looking at was a Replogle globe from the early eighties. A spastic thing, the globe was set at an angle well beyond the Earth's natural tilt, with a compass rose affixed to the South Pacific and a ketchupy stain over Kinshasa, in what was then known as Zaire. I spent many hours spinning that globe, an index finger poised over the Earth's thrumming surface, looking for somewhere to go. Eventually, I would memorize all the capitals of all the countries, the continents' high points and nadirs, but before geography became an object of study for me, the globe was just one of many props I recruited for endless games of make-believe. These games took place in my childhood home, in a room right above the garage we called the "bonus room." When I wasn't at school or rambling about outside, I would lock myself into that room with the globe, some books, and a purple physio ball I liked to dribble as I paced, its rhythmic bouncing operating like a metronome for my daydreams.

Years later, I would find the Wikipedia page for something called "maladaptive daydreaming," a non-*DSM*-listed compulsive behavior whose sufferers report daydreaming so vividly, their imaginations take over their daily lives, inhibiting the dreamer's ability to socialize with other people or focus on workplace tasks. While my own daydreaming certainly felt compulsive at times, having a story ready to go in my head was—for a child with excess time and few obligations—more boon than hindrance. I played out sprawling storylines in the finite space provided by the bonus room, stories of young and reckless love, martial arts mastery, epic odysseys across the Earth. My parents coined a term for these sessions. They called it my "locking door time."

Looking back at those years—and really, it was years until I stopped feeling the desperate urge to retreat into my mind—I realize I was already turning storytelling into a ritualized practice with its own idiosyncratic rules and tightly controlled setting. No daydream could begin until the door was locked and the blinds completely blinkered. Only then would the metronome start its count, the globe its wobbly revolutions. The purple ball would bounce, or my finger would land. I'd set off for Burma or Bhutan, passing through tessellated cities and particolored landscapes, turquoise gulfs and rivers running rampant, abandoned islets, searing steppes, all these spaces with no apparent relation to the American suburb that lay flat and deceptively silent outside my window.

⸻

I HAVE ALWAYS HAD TROUBLE DISTINGUISHING BIOGRAPHY from geography—the question of *who I am* always starts with a question of *where*. Maybe every life is just a string of settings through which one person proceeds. Or maybe a life is a set of places organized into a configuration that doesn't adhere to a linear path: these places that encase you, these other places that fill you with hope. In these ways and others, lives look curiously like maps to me.

I have never wanted marriage or children, great fame or fabulous wealth—but a life rich in geography, in places explored or vistas collected, that is something I have both wanted and tried to create for myself. In my mind, there are no drives or guiding clichés more potent than these: the need to map one's place in the world, the concomitant need to tell stories about those maps.

I suppose I absorbed much of this yearning from the stories I read as a child. The books I checked out from the library were filled with lady knights, handsome knaves, and farm girls who spoke to horses. Many of these books began with a map page, which for me was a nest of lines presaging adventure. Map pages sketch the worlds that authors create and that readers abscond to. What they portray is not a verifiable, geophysical location, but its opposite: a fabulist geography, a topos grounded in myth. (One early, iconic example of a map page precedes Thomas Moore's *Utopia*, a book whose titular setting famously doesn't exist.) At nine, my favorite book was J. R. R. Tolkien's *The Lord of the Rings*, a story that sent me traveling, sentence by sentence, from the Shire to Mordor and back again. Tolkien's map page achieved much more than helping me visualize Middle Earth; it lent a geographic structure to his tale of Manichaean struggle. Sauron's fell hordes originated in the East. The world of men and their allies, if it was to survive, would make its last stand in the West. Reading *The Lord of the Rings* situated me somewhere on that map. With every chapter, new sites were added and illuminated, until the book's entire plot had *taken place*.

The writer Guy Davenport, who once studied under Tolkien at Oxford, claims there is a "geography of the imagination" that must be considered alongside any geography of cities and landforms, glaciers, and bays. A geography of the imagination would include all those places that underpin our mental lives—places that, for writers and artists, give rise to the settings of novels and the backdrops to plays. When I was a child, any place external to the closed circuits of daily life—the school, the neighborhood, the bonus room above the garage—I thought of as my imagination's domain. I knew these other places to be real, or at least more real than the places I'd found in books, but just like with Middle Earth, I first accessed these places via the representational magic of storytelling, of maps.

After the Replogle globe lost its luster, I begged a subscription to *National Geographic* off my parents and began devoting much of my locking door time to flipping through that magazine's pages, enthralled less by the articles than by their pictures, which showed me Arizonan cliff dwellings, Indonesian reef reserves, Mexican cenotes, Namibian dune fields, Kamchatkan volcanoes. Each photograph came with a matter-of-fact caption, like "Women of the Wessex subdivision don tiaras at bunco princess night, a mix of dice game and costume party where moms can let their hair down." Unibrowed with vague concern, I also scanned into my brain *National Geographic*'s coverage of international crises, from

America's still-young wars in Afghanistan and Iraq to the latest quake in Haiti or famine in Darfur. I had no language back then for "the gaze," and did not understand—except subconsciously, perhaps—my favorite magazine's editorial messaging: how *National Geographic* divided an *us* (the homebound American reader) from a *them* (the foreign, beleaguered, but somehow attractive Other); how it did this by organizing the world into a series of beautiful disasters in my lap.

To map a place, to perform cartography's show-and-tell, one must choose what to include and what to leave out, seeking clarity in redaction. Perhaps this is why geography has long been the province of the surveyors and catalogers, the warmakers and orientalists—those who would show the world in order to control it. More personally, I fear that immersing myself in geography has really just been a means of avoiding people, of charting the scene while ignoring that scene's inhabitants. I associate it with locking door time: years in which I turned inward in order to project myself, or an idealized version of me, out.

All the hours I spent staring at maps certainly took my mind somewhere, but in other ways, loving geography made me stay put. It enabled my desire to recede, and turned me into a willing and delighted recluse. Ours was not a house animated by free-flowing conversation. My parents took care of me and my siblings, but also left us to our own devices. I would sometimes hear one of them approach the locked door of the bonus room and halt there, on the perimeter of my daydreams. I'd pause what I was doing and listen to them listening, our mutual curiosity never sharpening into intrusion.

IN 1988, MY MOTHER FLEW FROM SHANGHAI TO SEATTLE, AND later from Seattle to Chicago, Chicago to Tennessee, on board a

United Airlines plane. She'd shown up at Shanghai's Hongqiao airport dressed in a light blue raincoat, kelly green polo, and pink low-top sneakers. She'd packed plums for the flight, and now wasn't sure what to do with their pits.

My father had made the same trip two years earlier. In the interim period, my parents had done the long-distance thing, posting letters across the Pacific and speaking by phone when they could. He'd told her everything he thought she needed to know about America: that the exchange rate was four yuan to the dollar, that the portions were large and the houses larger, that the country smelled of gasoline and talcum powder, and that she'd get on fine as soon as she spoke the language. When my mother got to her first American apartment, she was surprised by the number of closets she now possessed. "I had to count them more than once," she told me. "The number just didn't make sense."

I used to think of her story every time I embarked on a trip. It was a kind of ritual for me, a kind of make-believe as well. What would it be like to lose the place I was leaving, to gain the place that I went? The geography of my imagination began with these two poles: one in China, one in America, and in between, a lissome thread of migration. Has that thread been anything less than the founding condition of my life? (A second son, I probably wouldn't exist if my parents hadn't left a one-child nation for the West.) Has the desire to retell their migration story not kept me tirelessly in motion, in between and out of step?

In 1997, I went to China for the first time. My parents were attending a conference in Hong Kong, after which they took my brother and me to the mainland. I have seen video evidence of me sitting atop a drugged tiger at the Hangzhou Zoo, my already big head dwarfed by the tiger's even larger noggin, but all I remember from that trip are the beverages: a chocolate milk I gulped down on an escalator, a can of Sprite handed to me on a cold, bright day.

I went again in 2006, 2008, 2009, 2010, 2012, and 2013. I was old enough by the first of these visits to know I was being sent to see the place my family was from, and I could guess by the last that this notion of perpetual return is, for many Chinese Americans, a powerful idée fixe. I began to feel caught in a loop: to visit China was to travel, setting out repeatedly for a place that wasn't my home, but it was also to "go back." With each return, I was maybe getting closer to my Chinese origins, to a version of myself antecedent to migration, unified and traceable. And yet the only way to seek out that version of me was to embark on so many trips, to keep on putting the map in play. The excursions I took to China fed into other trips, to other places. I became not a more Chinese person, but a person addicted to journeying, to feeling out of place.

I went back to China in 2014, and yet again in 2017, staying for a year each time. My assumption was that these lengthier trips would settle, once and for all, the matter of origination. But even then, I felt like I was looking for something—not a missing part of myself, but a way for the existing parts to fit together. I got so engrossed in taking these trips, in mapping my parts, that I eventually exhausted my love of geography, forgetting that places are there to be lived.

———

NOT LONG AGO, I FOUND MYSELF AT THE BOSTON MAPPARIUM, staring at an image of the world. Visitors to the Mapparium stand on a bridge bisecting a spherical room. The room's diameter is thirty feet, its one curving wall clothed in stained-glass panels depicting a map of the world from 1935, when the Mapparium was constructed and the world was a very different place.

Our guide reminded us of this world's particular prohibitions (no food, no beverages, no recording of any sort), and advised against leaning too far into the globe's inner void, as wedding rings and glasses had been known to take off for the Antarctic. "There are no secrets in the Mapparium," she told us, for voices carry strangely in spherical rooms. Standing on one end of the bridge, I could listen in on conversations happening on the world's other side—a whisper near Port Moresby delivered to an ear pricked by Cayenne. "Where's Dallas again?" "Mom's late." "I heard it's Boston's top-rated bathroom."

A kind of show happens every half hour inside the Mapparium. LEDs hidden behind the glass go on and off in a wavelike motion, simulating the sun's mobile curtain of light. A disembodied, feminine voice not unlike Sigourney Weaver's speaks from everywhere all at once. The voice gives the same spiel every day: something about the strength of our global community, something else about history bending toward justice, even some light admonishment of the vibrantly shaded empires, America's included, which by 1935 had colonized this map. At the end of the monologue, every visitor is asked to find that place on the map that they're from, the place they feel most connected to, and to recognize that place as part of a larger world that millions of people have tried over the centuries to safeguard and better.

A prompt-follower by nature, I quickly located the city where I lived (Boston), the state where I worked (Rhode Island), the country of my birth (America), and that of my parents (China). But the exact, peculiar, at turns close and distant place I was "from"—that locus appeared nowhere on this map. It was nameless, unmarked. "All the parts of the world are shown in their exact relation." Thus reads the Mapparium's legend.

In the late sixties, the urban planner Kevin Lynch conducted a study of what he called "cognitive mapping"—a term for how individuals turn spaces into usable mental pictures. Lynch asked thirty Bostonians to draw from memory the city in which they lived. Each mental map that resulted was different, shaped by its cartographer's social circles and habits, but certain landmarks, roads, and boundaries recurred, from the broad sweep of the Charles River to the State House's golden dome. Lynch hypothesized that the level of accurate detail in each mental map indicated how well situated its cartographer was in space and how connected they felt to their community. To have a map firmly in mind, to place oneself on its surface and share that plane with others. These were the prerequisites for flourishing in any place.

My introduction to the concept of "cognitive mapping" came courtesy of Fredric Jameson. There's a passage in Jameson's 1984 essay "Postmodernism, or, the Cultural Logic of Late Capitalism" that I can't stop thinking about, as it seems to diagnose not only the grand bewilderment of capitalism's latest, multinational phase, but also the state of psychic and physical drifting that for many years has characterized my life:

> So I come finally to my principal point here, that this latest mutation in space—postmodern hyperspace—has finally succeeded in transcending the capacities of the individual human body to locate itself, to organize its immediate surroundings perceptually, and cognitively to map its position in a mappable external world. And I have already suggested that this alarm-

ing disjunction point between the body and its built environment . . . can itself stand as the symbol and analogue of that even sharper dilemma which is the incapacity of our minds, at least at present, to map the great global multinational and decentred communicational network in which we find ourselves caught as individual subjects.

What Jameson was hoping to define was a time period, "late capitalism," in which our connections to specific places and people had grown frailer and more friable, stretched thin along transnational supply chains or diffused into mass-produced imagery like the sort published in *National Geographic*—a time in which the practice of mental mapping was all but impossible, because none of us knew where we were anymore, or how to get, unaided, from one place to another. In the decades since his essay's publication, as capitalism has gotten ever later, Jameson's basic argument has been reiterated in response to everything from climate change to the internet. Many people now believe that the map page has disappeared from everyday life, and that where we are is no longer a clearly physical phenomenon that geography—itself a nearly moribund discipline—can be counted on to assess. Being alive on Earth today, we're told, means being a body deprived of place, conscious only of the self and its avatars, each and every one of us lost in some irrevocable way.

As with any argument that aims to define an epoch, there is a degree of purposeful amnesia built into Jameson's thesis. If we are lost today in late capitalism's hall of mirrors, then I find it difficult to believe that the flaneurs of Baudelaire's day or the transcendentalist hermits of Thoreau's weren't similarly led astray, or that the many young men and women sent to the countryside by Mao weren't also pestering people for directions, or that a heightened degree of lostness can even be imputed to one time period over another. My beef is not with Jameson's essay, which he knew to be hyperbole with a grain of sense. My beef is with the corresponding assumption that late capitalist feelings can't also be deeply felt, or that this moment's trademark experiences of transit and flight defy all attempts at representation, at mapping.

I SLEEP TODAY IN A ROOM FULL OF MAPS. THE MAPS IN MY BEDroom show four cities where I used to rent an apartment, as well as a country I haven't visited in years. I like to think of these diagrams as after-maps, because they portray places I used to know, and because when I collected each map, I was trying to signal that place's completion in my life. But maps prophesize as much as they remember. My mother once told me a story of being one year out of college and marooned on an island off China's coast, teaching chemistry in a local college. One of her roommates in the teachers' dorm had pinned an English-language map of the world to their wall, and on nights when not very much was happening, the young women would challenge each other to name the capitals of foreign countries and locate them (at this game of maps, my mother apparently knew no equal). Some of these women would stay in China; some of them would leave for the places that they named.

In grade school, on the other side of that map, a teacher asked me to draw a picture of the neighborhood where I lived. I drew creeks and fields and lawns. I drew rows of brick houses framed by oak and tulip poplar. I drew the curving streets where my parents took their daily walk, the sprinklers unfolding their parabolas of watery light.

I'm not nostalgic for that place, not really. What I miss is the surety of that map page, the ease with which I prepared it, the pleasure and also security of knowing, without equivocation, my place. The suburban cosmos I laid down on that page had its own foundational fictions, of course (the "PRIVATE PROPERTY" signs; the heteronormative shtick of family above all else). And yet these fictions were home to me.

It wouldn't be long before I started probing at the edges of that map page, the shrunken sphere it delimited, even if that sphere was in America and America was—as relatives and teachers all reminded me—a happy, prosperous place. I wanted other Americas, other happinesses, other, chosen ways of feeling out of place. I wanted, too, to know that other Middle Earth: 中国, or the "Middle Kingdom," a place of the past I'd dog-eared for return. What did all those hours spent spinning a globe afford me if not this need to move past the maps I'd inherited? All along I was waiting for a new map to appear. I needed that map to be as detailed and forgiving as possible. I needed it to bleed into me, line by line, until its coordinates gave me my bearings, and its meridians told the way. The hope was always to go far, and for a story that looked like my own to commence.

KNOXVILLE/NUOCHENG, 1996

Take My Name but Say It Slow

Tom resumed his whitewashing, and answered carelessly:

"Well, maybe it is, and maybe it ain't. All I know, is, it suits Tom Sawyer."

"Oh come, now, you don't mean to let on that you *like* it?"

The brush continued to move.

"Like it? Well, I don't see why I oughtn't to like it. Does a boy get a chance to whitewash a fence every day?"

That put the thing in a new light. Ben stopped nibbling his apple. Tom swept his brush daintily back and forth—stepped back to note the effect—added a touch here and there—criticized the effect again—Ben watching every move and getting more and more interested, more and more absorbed. Presently he said:

"Say, Tom, let *me* whitewash a little."

Tom considered, was about to consent; but he altered his mind:

"No—no—I reckon it wouldn't hardly do, Ben."

—MARK TWAIN, *THE ADVENTURES OF TOM SAWYER*

My mother names me after the son of the doctor who delivers me. This is the early nineties, and the doctor wears a very white coat. Everything appears starched: the nurse's hair, the spic-and-span quadrant of floor, the doctor's timbre of voice, his white, white coat.

Mother has been here before. She sits sweaty and yet unflappable, her second delivery proceeding in a manner that deters reflection:

things are on their way, my father taking calls in the hallway, Clinton sweeping Arkansas, then Alabama, words and news building and subsiding, the good doctor talking a lot about names. Mother begins to push.

My deliverer has two sons: Tom and Jim. Either would make a fine American name, he assures my mother, even though there is no standard metric for such things. The name Jim already belongs to my mother's lab director, a man who reads to her as sweet but febrile. Tom, on the other hand, is clean of direct associations and yet rich in assumed cultural currency. My parents are newly aware of *Tom and Jerry*, and Mr. Tom Selleck from Hawaii, and when they were college students in Hangzhou, they must have read, in Mandarin first edition, of a Midwestern boy named Tangmu Suoya who went toe-to-toe with Injun Joe and kissed Becky's cheek by the wide, gracious Mississippi. They finish the paperwork, take their second son home to graduate housing, back into that May heat and the throes of my mother's dissertation, a body of work she will defend later that summer, seated before Jim and his cronies in an oxford shirt and wire-frame glasses, chemical formulae parting in uncertain spools from her mouth.

Months before I am born, my parents settle on a Chinese name, one chosen instead of borrowed. They will call me Nuocheng (诺成) in honor of my birthplace, Nuokesiweier (诺克斯维尔), or Knoxville. For the first few days, though, I have no name, at least not in the language I claim as my own today. My parents hold me, and pace. I cry only a little. They bathe me in their conversation, lathering my ears with their speech, the coo of each 诺 and each 成, these soft, gentle namings. On my wrist, a bright blue tag lists sex and mother's last name: *Boy, Luo.*

IN 2015, A CHINESE NAME WAS AT THE HEART OF A CONTRO-
versy in the literary world. At issue were three Chinese-sounding syllables, Yi-Fen Chou, and how these syllables had been used by a white
poet named Michael Derrick Hudson as his POC nom de plume.
Chou's poem "The Bees, the Flowers, Jesus, Ancient Tigers, Poseidon,
Adam and Eve," was selected by the Native American writer Sherman
Alexie for the 2015 edition of *The Best American Poetry*. When alerted
to this coup, Hudson wrote Alexie a note revealing his duplicity. The
poem Alexie had figured as the handiwork of an unknown Asian poet
was actually, *ta-da*, the brainchild of a Caucasian male archivist living
in Indiana.

As Alexie later wrote in a blog post on the *Best American Poetry*
website, "In the end, I chose each poem in the anthology because I
love it. And to deny my love for any of them is to deny my love for all
of them." The poem was republished, and if you purchase a copy of the
anthology today and flip to Hudson/Chou's contributor bio, you can
read about how "The Bees" was rejected by more than a dozen publications when submitted under Hudson's white name (he kept "very
detailed submission records") before eventually finding a home at
Prairie Schooner, and later *The Best American Poetry*, under the byline
Yi-Fen Chou. "If indeed this is one of the best American poems of
2015, it took quite a bit of effort to get it into print," Hudson/Chou
groused, implying that literary merit had, in the publishing landscape
of the day, been overlooked in favor of diversity quotas.

Like many Asian American writers with their own mostly unused
and out-of-print Chinese names, I found it hard not to take Hudson's gambit a little personally. I wondered why the poet instinctively

reached for a Chinese name when the time came to exotify himself, why yellow seemed like the most desirable, or convenient, shade. I wanted to ask Hudson some follow-up questions: Is it really so easy to write yourself thus pigmented? To play this game of charades because you have nothing to lose and much to gain in terms of accolades, and notoriety, and the embarrassment of liberal editors who, you believe, have rejected you as who you are, which is to say a white, entitled poet?

I was annoyed on many counts with Hudson and talked shit about him while eating tacos on multiple occasions, spilling salsa down my shirtfronts. But I also bore him a grudging respect, or at least recognized something of myself in him and his actions.

For years, I have set aside my own given, Chinese name in favor of one with Aramaic origins, a name my parents opportunistically took from a white doctor's family tree. I've done this in the interest of making my daily life more convenient, and by that metric, I've not had cause for regrets. Thomas gets me through the roll call quicker than Nuocheng. It is the name on my driver's license and passport, a word whose primary synonym in my head is *me*. Besides, I don't need to use a Chinese-sounding name to telegraph my heritage. General physiognomy, plus the American penchant for assigning racial identity at a glance, will almost always suffice.

When Michael Derrick Hudson jettisoned his given name to become Yi-Fen Chou, he was turning a trick that I and many other Asian Americans turned first—a Dai Nuocheng becoming a circumspect Thomas. Both choices, mine and Mr. Hudson's, evince a certain pragmatism, a hankering for results. Both involve a swapping of one name, deemed impractical, for the potentialities of another. As someone who sometimes regrets how easily I let my own Chinese name lapse, I admire Hudson for his pluck, the way he can take on a Chinese

name that roughly means a "piece of stink" and still end up in a pres-
tigious literary anthology, the way he is unashamed of all this. What
emerges is an odd brotherhood, a kinship I discern in the abandonment of given names and the adoption of aliases. It is this taxonomic
traffic that aligns us, that allows me to see him just as I see myself—
smudged, an incomplete erasure of heritage and color.

As for the poem itself, "The Bees" mostly contains twee imagery of
insects and flowers, but there's one line that sticks out to this reader,
a sad little riff on what it means to narrate one's life in "fractured
/ not-quite-right English." That "not-quite-right English" is perhaps
the only stereotypically Chinese aspect of Chou's poem. In his blog
post, Alexie parts the editorial curtains to explain that one of the
most important reasons he chose the poem was that it was written
by a Chinese-sounding person, yet "didn't contain any overt or covert
Chinese influences or identity." What most endeared the poem to
Alexie was the idea of "a Chinese American poet who would be com-
pelled to write a poem with such overt and affectionate European classical and Christian imagery."

Being Chinese in name but white at its pith, that is what elevated
Chou's work to "best."

———

DEPENDING ON THE SCENARIO, A NAME CAN BE EITHER A CATA-
lyst or a hindrance, a mark of pride or a lasting shame. Names are labels, little semantic handles we like to hold on to. But not every handle
fits its door, and some knobs even fall off if not properly installed.

George R. Stewart, in his study of North American place-names,
equates the names on maps with heritage. Toponyms accumulate over
time, connecting present-day Americans to our continent's contested

past. Contemporary maps are strewn with names taken from Indian tribes, Catholic saints, Danish landholders (the "Bronck" that gave us "the Bronx"), and English monarchs, as well as European attempts at translating Indigenous words into colonial speech, like the Spanish take on *Apalchen* that gave rise to Appalachia. While many of the older place-names referenced physical or meteorological conditions at the sites in question, conferring names where "the thing and the name were almost one," later names followed the protocols of Empire. Rivers like the Hudson were named for their "discoverers," though only after the English had routed the Dutch, who in their language called that river "Mauritius." Naming, Stewart reminds his reader, is serious business, even if we don't take it seriously all the time. Indeed, the act of naming can get away from us, until we find ourselves sowing them willy-nilly, splitting and joining and hyphenating ourselves into a kind of chaos.

As my mother well knows, scientists take a more meticulous approach. In the months that I grow, embryonic in her womb, my mother stays busy in Jim's lab, trying to modify a highly stable organic compound called adamantane into a more reactive form. The carbons in adamantane have a chair structure, a molecular shape similar to that of diamond. Chemical nomenclature always denotes a specific number, type, and arrangement of atoms. In trying to alter adamantane's structure, my mother is, in a sense, seeking to change its name.

She sees it clearly, this new molecule, swiveling in dreamy, chimeric geometries, its hydrogens coming and going, every name just a temporary dalliance, a label ready to be shed.

———

FOR THE FIRST FEW YEARS OF MY LIFE, MY PARENTS CALL ME "Cheng-cheng," and speak to me only in Mandarin. They're fresh out of grad school, and I have an older brother they call "Nuo-nuo" lying next to me in the crib. I remember the first day of kindergarten as the beginning of my American life: crying as I piss all over the toilet seat, suddenly having to speak English all the time. I walk to Bluegrass Elementary hand in hand with my nainai, who is dressed in paisley and Payless, her hair still black at the roots. The teacher calls me "Tommy Day," and over a red bin full of dried rice, I make my first friend, who is olive-skinned and ringlet-haired, seraphic, the most beautiful thing I've ever seen.

Back home, my yeye stands in the postage-stamp front yard, making a drawing in colored pencil of his son's first American house. My father has just started working at a state-run lab. My mother sits inside the drawing, slowly writing a paper about modified adamantane cages and waiting for certain names to stick: *Joyce the teacher; John the dentist; Dan who sold us this house; Tommy and David and Huimin pronounced the American way, like "human."*

The first house isn't big enough, so we move. I spend a long summer in an apartment in Oak Ridge while my parents drive around the valley, talking to realtors. The apartment has ladybug carcasses all over the sills and a mattress on the ground that my brother pushes me out of at night. One day, playing hide-and-seek with a girl in the neighboring unit, I accidentally shut myself into a utility closet and can't get out. The air inside is stale, rarely breathed, and for some time I sit in the darkness with the cobwebs, calling for my playmate. Panic seems like an option, but I am an oddly patient child, or so my parents tell me. I hear them now, my parents, returning from their daily walk, and already the darkness is opening up, the neighbor girl heading on home, the upstairs apartment and its miasmas receding. It is all so obviously temporary, a prelude to the big, airy house in the suburbs, to baseball-themed wallpaper left behind by the last family and my baby sister swaddled in shades of bubblegum pink.

In the new neighborhood, the boys and girls give me their own nickname, "Flat Face." Later, they'll call me "Tin-Tin" and my brother "No-No," riffing on our parents' pet names for us. My best friend at the time is three years older than I. He's cool and dauntless, a swimmer. Every Saturday, he calls the landline using an exaggerated Asian accent and asks if my mother is making fried rice again. I go over to his house. We drink cans of Coca-Cola in his darkened kitchen and play the World War II map on *Star Craft* through the night.

By high school, I am telling my mother to call me Tommy, not Cheng-cheng, and then Thomas, not Tommy-eh. My new best friend is blond and snarky and possibly gay, a proto-twink who calls me "Chinky." It's not important who comes up with this name. What's important is that this boy calls me anything at all, that he forms two syllables and means them for me. Weekend after weekend, the blond boy invites Chinky to sleep over at his house by the train tracks and a too-green lake, and now that he's been given this new name, Chinky becomes less invisible at school. He joins cross-country and helps his girlfriends pick out dresses at the West Town Mall. He does well in all his classes but doesn't make a big deal about it. The problem (and the fear) is always that other Asian kid on the bus with few friends and no name, not even an epithet. Chinky dislikes this Asian kid and disowns him before he returns the favor. When senior year superlatives come around, Chinky is nominated, like every other Asian, for "Most Likely to Succeed," but ends up winning "Best Dressed" instead, a change in the program notes which feels like validation.

But before all that, the blond boy turns sixteen and throws a party. A few weeks later, I stop talking to him, for reasons I can't grasp at first. My now ex–best friend tells everyone I gave him head under the covers that night, that he wouldn't have "let me" had he known I was going to take it so seriously. I'm pissed, but what I let him do is continue thinking this way, because the real shame is not sexual but lexical, and therefore difficult to put into language. The truth is, I've never liked this name, Chinky, which my friend manages to say with such affection. I can't believe how close I'd let the name get, seeping into my slushy sense of self. *My parents have heard him call me this*, I think, cringing. *They've seen me perk up like a dog, and run.*

And in the end, what happens? A chemical shift, a change in structure. I move north for college. The best friend of a boy named Chinky occasionally drifts into view, but always at some remove. A few years later, at a holiday party on the same Southern campus where my mother finished her doctorate, I straddle his lap and kiss him against a port-stained futon, but it means nothing to me—just another name I won't answer to anymore.

I READ ONCE IN A MARK TWAIN STORY THAT "FANCY IS NOT needed to give variety to the history of a Chinaman's sojourn in America. Plain fact is amply sufficient." The "facts" that Twain relates in his story are typical of early Chinese immigration to our country. Twain's protagonist Ah Song Hi, recently arrived from Shanghai, writes to his friend Ching-Foo of being beaten and kicked by police, mauled by dogs, thrown in prison, extorted for money he didn't possess, cursed and scratched by prostitutes, placed on trial but unable to testify on his own behalf, sentenced, and locked away. This litany of miseries feels rather distant from my own experiences, for the overall "facts" of Chinese migration have definitely changed, so much so that reading Twain's story as a Chinese American of my generation and class feels like encountering yet another projection of who I am—not a history lesson, but a yellow-tinted image on a white, white sheet.

My Chinese name, the one I was given but never use, also feels like that to me: an exotic gloss on a mostly assimilated product. I have never gone by Nuocheng and have no plans to do so, in print or in real life. Making a concerted effort to go by that name would feel like I was trying too hard, laboring to project a pure Chineseness I have never even come close to embodying.

I once met a man who came to my apartment and, mid-undress, asked me to tell him my Chinese name. Though I am usually wary of this question and the assumptions it makes, the man seemed sweet, and genuinely curious, and so I told him my name, as well as the logic behind it. I told him that Nuocheng combined the first character of Nuokesiweier—the Chinese isomer of Knoxville, Tennessee—with that of Chengdu, the metropolis in western China where my mother's family still lives. I told him that my brother, Nuoou, had been named in a similar fashion, with the *ou* referring to a river in my father's hometown of Wenzhou, while my sister, Nuohang, drew the second half of her name from Hangzhou, the city where my parents met and married. All three of us siblings, named for the places our parents were from.

In telling that story to a stranger, I realized something I'd known but never found interesting before: strip away our Chinese names' connotations of cultural difference, and what you are left with is a place, or rather a sequence of them, a topogeny. Topogeny is an anthropological term similar to genealogy. It describes a recitation not of ancestors, but of place-names important to a person, family, or clan. Sometimes topogeny and genealogy get mixed up, though, with family members named for places or places named after people. Among the Southwestern Hopi, the Rotenese of Timor, and many other Indigenous groups, topogenies function primarily as narratives of migration, tales bespeaking both settlement and flight.

"I like that," the man said. "I wish my name meant something more to me than just 'Patrick.'"

As Patrick and I did what we had come to do, little lights started going off inside me, points on a map I could finally see from above. What are place-names, asks the philosopher Michel de Certeau, if not "stars directing itineraries"?

———

WHEN I FIRST STARTED WRITING THIS ESSAY, I HAD THE IDEA IN my head that just like Hudson/Chou, I would write something that took on a Chinese name, one I'd never really used but nonetheless was mine. The story of this essay would thus be one of recovery, of an old and ethnic name excavated, preserved, and, at long last, claimed. But this isn't true to how I've lived with my names, always choosing the English one over the Chinese. Nor is it even true of my "Sinonym" itself, whose cultural and even linguistic roots are far from pure. Nuocheng is not a common or classical Chinese name (its primary referent, after all, is a mid-sized American city). My name translates the name of a non-Chinese place, but that place was also named for a man, Henry Knox, one of George Washington's right-hand men, who as far as I know never set foot in his namesake city. Continuing along this etymologic chain, I find that Knox is a common Scottish surname derived from the Gaelic word *cnocc*, or hill. And so my Chinese name really refers to a place named for a person named for a place, or rather, a generic type of landform, one likely familiar to residents of present-day Knox County, who sometimes think of themselves as hillbillies. Last comes the -ville, which is French in origin and means nothing more interesting than "town."

Whatever my feelings about Nuocheng/Nuokesiweier/Knoxville, I eventually left the part of the world that all these names inscribe. In college, I majored in biology and hung out almost exclusively with other Asians. Though I had no intention of racializing myself, I found I gravitated to people whose birth names also went unsaid, and who, like me, lived at least part of their lives in a different language. Those names and those languages did not haunt us, or if they did, we kept it to ourselves. What joined my friend group together was less a shared racial or cultural identity and more the comfort we felt in not having to perform our poorly articulated and hybrid identities to each other, not until we were ready to, at least.

One fall, as a break from my science classes, I enrolled in a course on Asian American literature taught by a Korean woman who'd recently earned her doctorate at Stanford. Professor Kim's reading list included the usual suspects (Maxine Hong Kingston, Chang-Rae Lee, Jhumpa Lahiri), but also names I hadn't seen before (Nam Le, Agha Shahid Ali, Charles Yu). There were just two non-Asian students in my seminar, and both of them spoke Chinese better than me.

Later that semester, as the dregs of Hurricane Sandy buffeted New England, I sat in an emptied dining hall with a friend, overanalyzing our classes. I filled her in on Professor Kim's class and how predictable I found its demographics, to which she responded that it was difficult for her (white and forcefully erudite) to see herself in "ethnic" literature. I sat on that comment for some time, trying to remember all the books I'd been assigned in high school English courses, the steady diet of Steinbeck, Hemingway, Chopin, Plath, Orwell, and Woolf.

I remembered how easy it'd been for me (Asian and bookish) to traverse certain imaginal boundaries—to wish myself into white bodies staring at lighthouses and kissing men named Alcée—and then I thought of all the names on Professor Kim's syllabus, the fact that I could barely think of any Asian authors she had missed. "I'm not saying it's not *good*," my friend hedged, "but it's definitely meant for a specific audience."

When college ended, I moved, predictably, to China, where all my family's names still pointed. Everywhere I went, people introduced themselves and asked to know my name. Thomas, I would say, pronouncing it "Toumasi." If they'd read any American literature in high school, as many of them had, they'd sometimes inquire: *Toumasi? Xiang Tangmu Suoya ma?*

Dui, I would respond, just like Tom Sawyer.

———

FOR SOMETHING SO PRIMARY, A NAME CAN FEEL, UNDER THE least bit of scrutiny, like a person's most arbitrary identifier. So why not cast them off? Out of the old names will surely arise a new cladistics. I think in the end what gets to me is how easily the new name came to him, how the white poet simply reached out and took one from the batch. There is something to be said for learning our names as we go, for treating them not as static forms, but as addresses we reside at only briefly. But still, it takes work, figuring a name. It's not something you can just steal from someone else, as Michael Derrick Hudson did with Yi-Fen Chou. You have to ease into it, this funny little domicile, and feel your way blind to its base.

According to a US State Department report, Mandarin is one of the harder languages for native English speakers to learn. This is partly because each syllable can be pronounced in many different ways, and can hold many different meanings. My name's Nuo is not just the Nuo of Nuokesiweier, my Cheng not just a callback to a city in China my mother grew up in. One of the professors who tried to teach me Chinese in college told me she'd assumed that the Nuo came from *nuoyan*, a phrase that translates to "promise," and the Cheng from *chenggong*, or "success." A name, she said, fit for strivers. Take my name but say it slow: a hometown, a mother city, a half-baked promise to succeed.

Tom gave up his brush with reluctance in his face, but alacrity in his heart.

BEIJING, 2014

The Figure a Trip Makes

I: THE IDEOGRAM

When I was twenty-two, I spent a year of my life just traveling. I was able to do this because I'd won a "purposeful travel" grant for recent college graduates. The grant was underwritten by a family of Boston Brahmins, shipping-magnate and art-collector types—the kind of people who believed in the importance of an adventurous and acculturated youth. I left for my trip in August 2014 and came back, almost exactly a year later, to Tennessee.

Past recipients of the grant, or so I imagined, had used the Brahmins' largesse to write their first novels in Addis Ababa or to hike every peak in the Tyrolean Alps. The project I applied to do seemed rather basic in comparison. I told the fellowship committee I would go to China and make a series of images of it: a year-long photo diary, half-image and half-text, documenting my stay in that country. I had this grand idea that my project would be a commentary on travel and transience as much as a study of China, and so I titled my diary *Neverwhere*; its contents, I posted to Tumblr.

To receive such a bequest at such an age can only scramble one's sense of what is practical and possible and what is not. While most of the people I knew were gearing up to enter that fig-leafed reaping machine I'd long spoken of, if never actually experienced, as "real life," I was being paid to take a trip. More specifically, I was being paid to follow a boy named Lucky out onto a frozen Manchurian lake, and to swim naked in the South China Sea after watching *Interstellar* in a theater shaped like a giant pineapple, and to write this all down on the bullet train to Xinjiang, weeks later, one temple against the window as sunlight beamed outside and oil derricks rose and fell in the distance, an audiobook of *I Wonder as I Wander* by Langston Hughes playing in my ear. I had no long view on the situation, no perspective. I was only twenty-two and, by trip's end, twenty-three. I had never filed my own taxes, nor traveled alone to a foreign country. Although I had some inkling of what I wanted to do with my life—write—I was still under the impression I had to *become* a writer first, as if the vocation preceded the act. My year abroad would be an initiation rite: I'd show up in China, go to as many places as I could, take a lot of pictures, and jot down copious notes. When I returned, I'd write a travelogue about it.

I knew about travelogues from reading *The Dialogic Imagination* by Mikhail Bakhtin, a Russian literary critic I once confused, in a bar, on a date, with the German philosopher Immanuel Kant. According to Bakhtin, not Kant, travelogues exist in an "extratemporal hiatus," an interval set apart from so-called "real life" and therefore alien to real life's rules and rhythms. Travelogues take place somewhere and *sometime* else. They convey not just a sense of physical distance, of places far, far away, but of temporal remove. When we travel, a rift forms inside of biography, and out of this gap extends an alternative timeline, what Bakhtin calls "adventure time," a timeline customarily defined by unprecedented events and fortuitous encounters.

Bakhtin was writing about the classics—Greek and Roman "adventure novels of ordeal" for which Homer's *Odyssey* may have served as inspiration. Such travelogues often relate the exploits of singular heroes. The trips they describe are long and laceratingly difficult, not to mention beset by frequent encounters with the supernatural and divine. In contrast, during the year in which I learned to travel, an estimated 1.1 billion people also left their country of residence to visit another. Travel on such a scale is better characterized as an industry than a quest, and for that year at least, traveling was also my job, a task I performed without any input from meddlesome demigods— unless you counted my Chinese mother, my grandparents, the friends and acquaintances who hosted me, and all the many strangers (flight attendants, customs officials, KFC shift workers and hostel receptionists) who variously helped or hampered my progress.

I note these distinctions because they are true, but equally true were my youth and my excitement. I believed back then in the epiphanies dealt by fern fronds and LSD; I also believed—and not in some ironic way—that I'd embarked on a quest, the quest to become a writer, and I believed this even as contravening evidence accrued. The majority of my adventure time consisted of repetitive, touristic activities, not aesthetically charged feats of derring-do. I ate meals prepared in *Lonely Planet*–approved restaurants. I went on walks. I looked at scenery I'd probably already previewed on Google or Baidu. There was some fun to be had from all this going down in a foreign place, with foreign-looking people milling in my periphery, and foreign-sounding voices percolating through the foreign-smelling air, but what actually made my trip feel special to me was the narrative I was even then trying to make of endeavor. Travel took ordinary life and laminated it, imparting this formal feeling, this fantasy of a plot. *I went somewhere. I came back.*

———

WHERE DID I GO THAT YEAR? TIANXIA, OR "ALL UNDER HEAVEN."

I went to Beijing, and I went to Shanghai.

I went to Lijiang and Dali, Huashan and Huangshan, Dunhuang and Shangri-La.

I went to Shenzhen, where, after a week of lying in bed, eating supermarket sushi, I walked across the border to Hong Kong.

I went to Changsha to inquire about a burning sensation. After two days spent loitering about the hospital's venereal disease department, queuing in lines that, when the doctors opened their doors, turned into scrums, I was discharged with a tube of antibiotic ointment and a box of mysterious capsules whose list of ingredients I photographed and sent to my mother for translation. "It's just turmeric," she told me.

I went to Guiyang, Kunming, Haikou, Guangzhou, Hangzhou, Chengdu, Xi'an, Changchun, Harbin, Lanzhou, Xining—a collection of provincial capitals.

I went to some places merely as a pretext for reaching someplace else—Kashgar as a means to Tashkurgan, for example.

I went to Dandong to lay eyes on North Korea, Heihe to do the same with Russia. In both cases, the other side of the river looked dour and nondescript. I saw a rusting fence and a cadaverous cellphone tower. I saw a Ferris wheel, kites, a pair of tiny people walking their tiny bikes.

I went to Taipei seeking some critical distance on China, or at least that part of China my relatives call the "*dalu*" (大陆), a phrase mean-

ing "continent" or "mainland" that I used to think was written 大路,
or "the big road."

I went to Manila to get out of Taiwan, Kuala Lumpur as a break
from the Philippines. Having well and truly spilled past the bounds
of my project proposal, I revised its description accordingly. "Documenting China" became "getting a sense of the Sinophone world."

I went to Tagaytay and saw a volcano inlaid with a lake, my body
on a boat cutting toward its center.

I went to Kathmandu with a friend from college. Our inbound
flight had to make an unplanned landing in Varanasi due to
weather conditions over the Himalayas—the worst turbulence I've
ever experienced. It had been a bad year for international aviation.
Planes had gone down in Indonesia, Ukraine, and the Alps. When
we landed safely at Tribhuvan Airport in Nepal, the entire cabin
stood up and cheered.

I went to New Delhi by plane, Osh by semi-truck, Tiger Leaping
Gorge and Nagarkot by foot. Almost everywhere else by train or by bus.

I went to a few places simply by going to a station and boarding
the next available bus. The whitewashed villages around Wuyuan
occurred to me in this way. So too the dunes of Zhongwei, the eel-
topped rice in Kaiping, the Yellow River as it winds blue and unstop-
pable through Guide City, the flat immensity of Qinghai Lake.

I went to Tongren to wait in line at the ATM as the monks typed
in their PINs.

I went to the toilet right as the train stopped in Turpan, all those
grapevines climbing the pergolas.

I went to Hohhot and did very little besides sit around Anda
Guesthouse, binging the fifth season of *Girls*. On one of my rare trips
out, I stopped to watch a runway show at the Grassland Silk Road

Cultural Park: gaunt models in bandage dresses carrying memory-foam pillows across a blue-lit stage.

I went to Sanya to pick up pretty rocks on the beach.

I went to Emei Shan and bowed before Samantabhadra.

I went to Xiamen, Ningbo, Chisapani, Bishkek, Zunyi, Taichung, Tunxi, Yinchuan, Songpan—each a stopover I no longer recall.

I went to so many places, and then I went to places within those places, like a botanical garden in Xishuangbanna, or a foreign concession planted with fake tulips in Tianjin, a Kyrgyz consulate in Ürümqi, a viewing platform by Sun Moon Lake, a stone tower inside Chishui's Bamboo Sea, where I followed the muddy footprints to the top of the stairs. (The footprints were somehow on the underside of the stairs.)

I went to San Francisco for a job interview, but didn't get the gig.

I went to Kuching because I'd been dreaming, all December, of rain. It was the wet season in Borneo, and the warren of streets outside my hostel had flooded, calf-deep. After the waters receded, I ran through the city on sidewalks covered in cracked rambutans and the oily excretions of cats.

I went to Bako National Park for a few days. A ranger in the canteen told me about his mistress's most recent miscarriage. "Right into the toilet," he said, making a flushing gesture with his hands. Later, he took me to see the proboscis monkeys in the mangroves. We watched them clamber down from the trees and disappear into the marsh.

I went to Wenzhou and took my place in my paternal family's tableau. The photographer kept telling us—my grandparents, my cousins, my aunts, my uncles, me—to squeeze closer together. "Act like you like each other," he joked.

I went to Chongqing with my mother because we wanted to go

THE FIGURE A TRIP MAKES

somewhere neither of us had ever been. We ate at a dumpling shop near the base of Nanshan, touristed our way through Ciqikou flea market, the Yangtze River docks, and that compound where the Chinese Communist Party and the Kuomintang signed a few important, but ultimately frivolous, documents long ago. At each juncture, I had my mother lead the way, for I could not read the signs.

I went to an island called Zhoushan where, in the early eighties, my mother taught chemistry before returning to the big road. She and I were the same age when we first came to that island, an alignment I found cosmically significant. Like that had been her gap year, her "extratemporal hiatus," and this one was mine. Like I was somehow continuing on the grounds of her leaving, building my trip forward while taking hers back. Some of my mother's old friends still lived on the island, but I stayed at the Holiday Inn.

I went to Yangshuo alone, Hailar alone, Jiayuguan alone, Qingdao alone, Karamay alone, Hoxtolgay alone, etc. "Do you think you'll be lonely?" a member of the fellowship committee had asked me at my interview. "I think there's a difference between solitude and loneliness," I'd said in response. "One is self-contained, the other one is needy." I would travel long enough that year to often forget the difference.

I went to Xiahe and met a gray billy goat, sulfur-eyed and unkempt. Three years later, what I remembered of that town had all been renovated or demolished, the sole holdover my goat.

I went to Karakul Lake and discovered the sense to a passage by Yoko Tawada: "I always wrote a travel narrative before I set off on a trip, so that during the journey I'd have something to quote from. I was often speechless when I traveled."

I went to Guilin and Langmusi and Wulong: a trifecta of greens.

I went to Jiuzhaigou to participate in the crowds.

I went to Arslanbob to see the world's largest walnut forest. I lay down in that grove, did not budge for hours, ate sunflower seeds and read Rimbaud out loud on my Kindle, jacked off, then left.

I went to Istanbul at the invitation of a friend. There was no easy way for me to contact them after landing, but I'd written their work address down in my journal. After getting off the bus in Taksim, I moved with the crowd until I found the exact cross section of the city my friend had described to me: a falafel stand beside an Italian restaurant, and in between, a cardamom-colored door. So many places had passed through each of us since last we met, but when I called up to their window, they immediately knew my voice.

I went to Changbaishan, the Ever White Mountain, and though ill-prepared, I made it through the drifts.

———

CHINESE TRAVELERS OF OLD OFTEN ENGAGED IN A PRACTICE known as *moya*, or "to polish a cliff." After arriving at an important destination, a traveler would carve a short poem or dedication into the rocks, leaving behind this commemorative text. Present-day visitors to sites of pilgrimage like Taishan in Shandong Province must literally pass over the words left by earlier travelers, messages that can only be read in situ, the characters as stationary as their makers were mobile. In this way, Chinese places are not just written of, but written on.

As I traveled, I kept multiple forms of record. I took photographs of the red steel scaffolding at Panjiayuan Market in Beijing, a delivery boy looking at his phone in Taipei, a rack of drying fish resting down an alleyway in Hainan. In my journals, I developed a passion for list-making, writing down everything from the distances between waypoints to the random items I'd lost along the way, as if even the missing bits of my trip needed to be retained. All of it, every iota, demanded some accounting: the famous sights, or *jingdian*, that I visited and my off-the-cuff impressions of each; what it said on billboards and signs ("Once Again You Are Welcome to Arrive the Nativity" and "Youth: Go Take a Trip with Your Heart"); all the "experiences" I'd recently had which seemed, after I wrote them down, like they'd happened to somebody else.

> 4/28/2015: There's an American film playing on the hostel
> television. Matthew Thomas of Christchurch, New Zealand is
> sprawled on the shag carpet waiting for the disc to stop freezing.
> His hair is down, frizzed out into a brownish thicket. His feet,
> like mine, are covered in sand. "I'm going to take you some-
> where beautiful," the man in the white dinner coat says, before
> the disc stalls once more.

It would be a stretch to call much of this "writing"—it was stenography. My hope was to produce a useful transcript for the writer I'd eventually become, an armory of details with which he'd outfit his travelogue. I even maintained a spreadsheet tallying every single one of my daily expenses, as if knowing that, on November 27, 2014, I spent ¥131.30 ($21.35), and that three of those yuan had gone toward a fried dough stick and a cup of warm soy milk, could possibly matter to the overall arc of my trip.

That story, its first draft at least, was already being written: my photo diary, my *Neverwhere* blog, the raison d'être of my trip. Whenever I fell behind on my entries, I would hole up for a few days in a room at the nearest 7 Days Inn, editing images and typing away on my laptop. I'd sometimes work all day and into the night, only stopping when a deck's worth of calling cards, each one printed with a different image of a sexily submissive Chinese girl, had accumulated under my hotel room door. I would gather up each of these cards, inspecting their pendulous offerings, the nubile silhouette of possible intimacy, and then consign them to the bin before heading out for a bite.

The mini-essays I wrote for *Neverwhere* ranged far and wide across China and its neighbors. Even still, my writerly gaze rarely left my navel. I was trying all the time to set the scene, and yet the scene was constantly shifting, whereas the first person "I" remained relatively stable.

I wrote, from Shangri-La, "I am staying in a guesthouse covered in prayer flags with a courtyard outside and a nice wooden terrace where one can stand and ponder the burnt embers of what used to be Shangri-La's Old City. There are no other guests here, and at night I can hear the owner and her lean, attentive boyfriend grunting through different positions downstairs."

I wrote, from Sanya, "The sea turtles are staying at the Ritz, in a shallow saltwater pool shaded by a thatch roof."

As far as I knew, only my mother and J, a French guy I'd met and slept with one night in Shanghai, were keeping up with these dispatches. My mother liked the pictures and didn't comment on the text. J, on the other hand, once sent me an email with the slightly ominous postscript, "And don't forget that I read your blog!"—a reminder that my wanderings weren't going unnoticed.

J sent me lots of emails that year, as well as the occasional WeChat text. He lived with his partner in Shanghai, who didn't know anything about me, which made our communiqués feel ill-advised, and he spoke English as a third language, which made our messages more considered and deliberate, at least on his part. "I guess we have already talked about most of what needed to be said about our relationship," he once wrote to me, "but I was being really dumb sometimes and also that language barrier that, yes, still exists may have left misunderstandings (delicate situations require to choose exact words and I tended to approximate a lot for lack of vocabulary)."

I found myself approximating a lot, too, when trying to describe how I felt about J. To call our time together an affair seemed overdramatic—we only saw each other a total of four times. But what else could I call it? A dalliance? A nonplatonic friendship? The truth is, I thought about J constantly as I traveled; he became, without much competition, my traveling self's invisible partner—the one person I'd genuinely "met" in all that time abroad, and moreover, someone who'd gotten to know me on the trip's inside and not before or after, who'd managed to find me in that most transitory phase. J seemed both impressed by the variousness of my travels and alert to when I was faking it—like when I tried on the hardened backpacker's posture of seen-it-all-before ennui. Meanwhile, I thought of him as a grown-up person with a real job and real life experience (Parisian upbringing, a research stint in the tropics), someone who was ostensibly settled but in a country not his own, an émigré not unlike my parents. I sent J long emails transcribing the minutiae of my trip—he didn't balk at how exuberantly I faced the world, how much I wanted to be a part of it. I felt both comforted and driven by his regard, a regard which felt all the more miraculous to me because its source remained at least partially mysterious. Seen, but not held, by J's attention, I pushed myself to travel to more and more places, to experience and then integrate, like some kind of peripatetic amoeba, all these beautiful and perplexing and breathtaking things that J might also love to see and be arrested by.

Of course I never told him any of this. I played it cool, or rather, I played the role dictated by our not-affair's circumstances: he the experienced expat and entrepreneur with his partner and his business; I the insatiable ephebe, ten years younger and wild with ardor. This approximation suited us, I thought; it had the markings of a familiar story.

Half a year passed in the course of a few rendezvous. J told me, on a park bench in Shanghai, that he was starting to feel guilty about our "situation." We decided to meet up in Xi'an with the express purpose of ending it, of getting out of one trip by way of another. He booked us into a hotel whose archaic facade was much grander than its interior. There was a red neon lamp on the nightstand, enclosed in a wooden lampshade ornately patterned with camellias, and in the bathroom, a metal showerhead dangling limply on its hose. We spent most of one afternoon circling the city's reconstructed walls, from when Xi'an had been Chang'an, and then walked together through the smoky Muslim quarter, snacking on quail eggs and brothy noodles. At night, we slept in the same bed, but did not touch. He told me that emotional entanglement had cowed sexual desire. He told me that *love* was a word now approximate to our condition, and because of that, we were finished.

I said very little in response to this disclosure, even though mine was the language we used for all our conversations. Later, he would tell me, in an email, that my reticence had come across as uncaring, callous. He regretted using the "big word," he wrote to me, and had only used it for want of suitable alternatives. "Since I came back from Xi'an," he wrote, "it feels like everything around, everything belonging to my current life, is outdated, worthless, and as if everything that revolves around you is exactly the opposite: in short, a bright, sunny future." He wrote further that a close friend of his had told him to leave Shanghai behind, throw caution to the wind, and join me on my trip. It was difficult to tell what J wanted from me: a relationship, or to take my place on the big road. He wrote to tell me that he couldn't help "identifying" with my life, even as I had no idea what there was to identify with. In my mind, he was the fleshed-out one; I was just a line not yet disciplined into a shape, a traveler looking to polish a cliff.

In Xi'an, before we checked out, I spread myself in a flat plane down his back, matching forearm to forearm, kneecap to kneepit, as if I might soak up each available inch of touch. Our plan, compiled weeks earlier, had been to climb a mountain called Huashan a few hours east of the city, and so we did it, climbing the stairs until they grew too steep for comfort, until both of us reached for the chain, hauling ourselves up a near vertical rise, matching each other's pace as our breath crystallized in the air, making it to the top, stopping.

HALFWAY THROUGH THE TRIP, MY MOTHER CAME TO VISIT. SHE wanted to travel with me in China, something we hadn't ever done together as a pair. She also wanted to take me to Chengdu so we could stay with my maternal grandparents, Apo and Agong, as they celebrated Chinese New Year. It was wintertime, and I had just come back from a heady month in Southeast Asia. J and I were in the middle of negotiating our endpoint. My mother only wanted to talk of beginnings.

Our mother-son tour group proceeded in rapid order from Hangzhou to Chongqing, and then from there to Chengdu. Traveling with my mother, who doesn't drink, or eat out, or shop with any seriousness (she's always liked deals, not purchases), was admittedly boring, but it was also a relief to no longer be plotting my own course, to hand my trip's reins over to someone else. Mom didn't want to eat the famously spicy hot pot in Chongqing, so we didn't. She was dubious about the quality of meat in China, so we subsisted on bananas and pomelo. I sensed her mood shift when we got to Chengdu—a city she'd lived in through her adolescence and the first place she'd ever set out from on her own. Mom got, dare I say, pensive, even sentimental. The year of the horse was about to become the year of the sheep, and my mother was back under her own mother's roof, looking disdainfully at the blue and gray curtains in the living room that hadn't been washed since the eighties, the mismeasured drapes my apo clothespinned shut each evening before bed.

On New Year's Eve, I asked my mother to tell me what it was like growing up here, and how it felt now to return. (I was very taken, at that point in my trip, by the image of a closed loop, and was hoping my mother would supply it.) We only came here because the factory your agong worked in got moved from Shanghai, she began to say, in English-flecked Mandarin. Actually, your agong lived here alone at first, and would ride the train back to see us when he could. Apo resisted leaving Shanghai. Even now, she likes to complain this whole province has nothing in it. But her mother, your great-grandmother, didn't think it was good for Apo to live apart from her husband, which I always thought was strange, because your great-grandmother never lived well with men.

She didn't get along with Apo's dad, you mean? I asked, interjecting. The two of us were walking in circles around a former amusement park, gazing up at the tracks of a decommissioned roller coaster.

Apo's dad died when she was five years old, Mom said, during the war with Japan. His body was separated into five parts, so they buried him in those pieces. Apo's mom got remarried to this guy in Shanghai whose family had no money, and your grandmother went to live with her uncle, who did have money, and always liked Apo, but then the Cultural Revolution was starting, and so he committed suicide. I don't really remember any of this, Mom told me, but Apo would always say to me that I should have my own job when I grew up and not depend on men, or I'd end up just like my grandmother. My grandmother was short but very pretty, and I think Apo didn't like that because everyone, even her own mother, liked to say that good looks skipped generations. When Apo brought me here so we could finally be with Agong, your great-grandmother and her son from her new marriage came as well. We all lived together in what was called the "Xinggongfang," or "New Apartment." Agong couldn't stand your great-grandmother because she was terrible with money and would always buy me and my brothers candy and other snacks that were, how do you say, forbidden?

I think you mean wasteful, I said.

Yeah, it was a waste. She liked to waste, and she also never backed down when Agong confronted her about it, and so we were known all around the apartment building as the family that liked to fight. It's funny because I don't actually think it affected me that much. I spent a lot of time outside back then. Until I turned fourteen, my friends all said I acted like a boy, always fighting with them, like physically, and often losing. I remember there was a little river beside the New Apartment. I would do things back then like dig a hole in the bank and fill it with water and leaves, so many leaves that it looked just like the ground in autumn, and then I'd wait for some people to walk by, and always someone would step into the hole, and be really angry, and there I was on the other bank, trying not to laugh.

———

I STAYED ON A WHILE LONGER IN CHENGDU, HOPING TO DRUM up content for my project. Most nights found me huddled at a cluttered table shoved into the entryway of my grandparents' apartment, staring at the peach motif on the floor's cracked tile and scribbling in my journal. An old rat had taken up residence in the wash closet, and dozens of cockroaches—ebony-colored and much more gregarious than the ones I was used to from the States—had the run of the kitchen. I was trying, as ever, to capture it all as it happened: my sleeping agong's labored breathing; the midnight prayers of his insomniac wife; the pink plastic bag she told me to put my underwear in whenever I used the shower; the shower whose drain doubled as our toilet and Agong's ashtray; my mother's lamentations about the curtains.

I could tell there was something different to this leg of my trip—different, but also the same. Here in Chengdu, my Bakhtinian travelogue had run aground on a family story, though maybe the family story was also the basis for my travelogue. Why else had I selected China for my year of "purposeful travel" if not to flirt with this narrative of return: the immigrant child's inherent "purpose" of one day reclaiming his roots? And yet, like so many returnees before me, I had come back to find a different country than the one my parents had left, a country of newfound economic mobility where nearly every building dated to 1980 or later, and where more concrete had been poured between 2010 and 2013 than during the entire twentieth century in America. I also came back underequipped to navigate any of these developments. (Good looks are not the only things that skip generations.) I could see China, but only from the outside, as a tourist might. Although my parents had raised me to speak, or at least understand, Mandarin, I never learned to read or write the language. All I really recalled from Chinese Sunday school were the different strokes used to compose each Chinese character: the lateral cut of a *heng* and the vertical fall of a *shu*, the willful wrist flick that makes for a *pie* and the delicate uptick of every *gou*. I could remember the manual aspects of crafting Chinese characters, of strokes migrating down my hand and onto the page, but none of the words' meanings. Because I'd mislaid my skills of decipherment, China did not speak to me in full sentences; China was endless form with no

content. Karst promontories carved by rain. A panel of fuchsia silk. Motes of cotton falling like meltless snow on the desert. A stone quay jutting into waves.

WESTERN SCHOLARS OF THE EAST USED TO THINK OF CHINESE writing as a mystical sign system independent from speech. While all English words are arrangements of letters, each of which is connected to a sound that, when strung together with other sounds, might result in a word with a meaning, Chinese words appear to represent their definitions more directly, much as a painting or a photograph does. Sinologists called Chinese characters "ideograms": signs whose meanings are indivisible from their graphic form on the page. For orientalists like Ernest Fenollosa, to write in Chinese was to deploy "much more than arbitrary symbols." The character 鳥, for example, refers intuitively to "bird": it looks beaked and winged, if not feathered. The word spelled "b-i-r-d," on the other hand, represents an utterance that users of one language, English, have established by group fiat to mean "avian." The former is a "vivid shorthand picture of the operations of nature," the latter a semantical appellation upon the real.

Unsurprisingly, this theory of a writing system whose transmission of meaning was as pure and unredacted as nature itself appealed to artists as much as scholars. Western poets like William Carlos Williams and Ezra Pound were heavily influenced by the idea of the Chinese ideogram. These poets were not trying to write poems in Chinese; they merely hoped to emulate the ideogramic properties of Chinese characters in English, to pioneer a poetry undifferentiable from its material basis ("no ideas but in things"). Pound edited and helped publish Fenollosa's seminal essay "The Chinese Written Character as a Medium for Poetry," which Pound called "a study of the fundamentals of all aesthetics." In that essay, Fenollosa argues that non-Chinese poets should learn to do "consciously what the primitive races did unconsciously," composing in a language drawn from the natural world, from mud and water, sticks and stones, rays and half-light. Chinese ideograms conveyed meaning organically, much like the Chinese themselves. They were "alive and plastic," naive and uncontrived. They evolved over time, these mutable shapes cleft from nature, but they also preserved their "primitive sap," that vitalist spark that set the word 火 aflame. Fenollosa hailed the "pictorial method" of Chinese characters as the "ideal language of the world." If we writers of English could only harness that "vivid figure," then we, too, could write sentences "like the mingling of the fringes of feathered banners," with words that glowed as bright as any sun.

Latter-day Sinologists have critiqued Fenollosa's writings as yet another projection of the Westerner looking east. After all, Chinese characters are only mute pictures for those of us who don't know the sounds attached to each character. That these ideograms careen through time and space, silently bearing meaning on their crenellated backs, is a conjecture highly susceptible to a kind of negative confirmation bias—we hear what we want to hear, but there are things we could never listen for in the first place. During my year abroad, I, too, dreamed, in my own Chinese illiteracy, of mastering the language of my forebears—or rather, the language of my forebears as already dreamt by orientalists. I came to believe that a language pulled directly from nature was the only possible way of capturing the immediacy of travel, and maybe if I tried hard enough, I could write an English-language account of my trip that worked like a Chinese ideogram, an intricate crosshatching of strokes that could suture ten thousand signifiers to their signifieds and eighty places to their names. Each time I've tried to write this essay since, I've been stymied by the unreasonable standard of an ideogramic language, these words that hug phenomena as tightly as any skin. You might say that the impossibility of me writing this travelogue has become oddly analogous to the impossibility of me ever writing in Chinese.

One evening in Chengdu, my apo handed me two albums full of photographs. I asked Mom to stay up with us for a while, and she told me what she remembered about different photographs and their occasions, helping me unmute the images. I noted the different perms she and my uncles used to sport and held up to the light flimsy negatives of my grandparents' identification photos. There was one photograph of my mother that struck me, ideogramically. In it, she stands on the beach in Zhejiang, looking directly into the camera as, behind her, the Pacific froths into a white line of foaming tension and pressure. My mother dated this photograph to just a few days before she left China for America, a detail that immediately piqued my interest. Here in the frame was the most comprehensive version of who she was before her life entered the genre of travelogue: before a trip had been imprinted on her, forming the output I knew from an input I could barely fathom.

I took a photograph of the picture, and carried it with me the rest of the way.

OVER THE COURSE OF THAT YEAR, IN NO SMALL PART BECAUSE I thought it might impress J, I began reading a lot of translated French theory on the internet: Gaston Bachelard, Deleuze and Guattari, Michel Foucault, and Michel de Certeau. It was de Certeau who taught me that "Every story is a travel story—a spatial practice." In his essay "Walking in the City," de Certeau theorizes a mode of writing—also mystical, potentially even ideogramic—that people perform as they travel. This is the writing made by a human body as it moves across a given space, what de Certeau thinks of as a traveler's "speech acts," their way of communicating nonverbally with the world. Every trip is composed of countless such acts, all coming together to tell a "spatial story," an unsayable and unwritable, but doable unit of language that elongates with every visit to a new city, every elision of a speeding rickshaw, every run-on-train-ride-cum-sentence terminating in a depot full of fortune tellers and pigeons. Places, for de Certeau, are really just the accumulation of spatial stories: all these instances when a person used their entire body like a pen.

After reading de Certeau's essay, I started to think that J and I had met like that, like a new city had sprung up from our meeting. This occurred during the second month of my trip. I'd been in Shanghai maybe a week, searching, without much conviction, for the site of my mother's old apartment, the one she and Apo had shared before the move to Chengdu. I knew it had to be somewhere near the Nanpu Bridge, in one of the lanes between Fuxing and Lujiabang Roads. I bet you anything it's gone, Mom told me. I sent her pictures of a bus station in her old neighborhood and giant parking lots blanketed in orange rubble—with the cheeky caption "Maybe you lived here."

J was working the till at his café in the French Concession when I walked in and ordered an Americano. It was raining outside, a deluge that had lasted for days. I sat shivering in my soaked linen shirt as he fixed me coffee and a bowl of mushroom soup. Afterward, we made pleasantries and stared at one another.

My mother says that Shanghai, for her, is Zhongshan Park in summertime, Yu Garden in winter, the view of a still-rural Pudong from her side of the river. When I think of Shanghai, I think of the plane trees that line the streets of the French Concession, their mottled bark tracing archipelagoes of nude and umber, and the particular way their leaves cut and origami the light. On the same day I met J, I paid a visit to the Urban Planning Exhibition Center in People's Square, where I got to see an enormous, room-sized model of Shanghai while listening to a cover of "Moon River." All of the important landmarks, from the Oriental Pearl Tower to the China Art Museum, had been rendered here in miniature. The model's layout is even continually revised to reflect new construction. Major projects that have been approved by city planners but not yet started still appear on the map, as if holding space for the future.

For some urban tourists, this is the view that matters: a city's parts fused into one whole, simultaneously expansive and detailed. Such a vantage point gives only a "fiction of knowledge," writes de Certeau. The true traveler is always rushing to take the elevator down from the observation post, to lose himself to the city and not its map, to be one of those flaneurs whose "bodies follow the thicks and thins of an urban 'text,'" and whose devotion to a place is "as blind as that of lovers in each other's arms." I wanted to be in Shanghai's arms, to know a strange and yet familiar city's open-ended embrace. That night, J took me to a wine bar just off Yongkang Road. He was up front about having a partner—a man he loved, a man he'd moved to China for—but was careful to also mention that his partner was away on business. I told him of my travels, of where I'd been the week before (Wenzhou) and where I was headed the week after (Changsha). We sat at the wine bar until it closed, waiting for either bravery or heedlessness to strike. De Certeau writes, of all those wanderers in the city, "They are no more inserted within a container than those Chinese characters speakers sketch out on their hands with their fingertips."

I downed my glass of red and sketched my intentions on J's palm. He took me home on the back of his bike, my arm slung around his waist, my sandaled feet floating above yards of slick pavement. That season's long rain was finally ending, and so we carried it all back with us: the just-washed summer air, the bike's rickety musculature, the people sleeping and wanting above the street.

We wrote the city, and the city wrote us free.

I CANNOT SAY PRECISELY WHEN AND WHERE I LOST THE PLOT, when I abandoned myself to motion. A strong possibility is early June: coming back into the physical and social isolation of Xinjiang after an almost too-magical reunion with a friend based in Asia Minor. In Istanbul, I'd somehow lost track of a bag with most of my journals from the trip inside, and despite telling myself that it was okay, that losing one's record is preferable to losing one's health or one's mind, I was distraught at the thought of my misplaced verbiage, all those thousands of words I'd laid down to turn myself into a writer. Also around this time, I woke up in the middle of the night to a loud battering at my door. Three police officers, two Han and one Uyghur, barged into the tiny room I was renting and crowded close to my bed. They looked at my laptop, my camera, my external hard drive, my passport, and asked me in an oddly parental way to explain what I was doing there, in an informal guesthouse by the Karamay bus station, with orange skins scattered across my sheets. I had just been passing through, I told them, playing dumb; I arrived so late I forgot to register. They told me I was too young to be out here on my own, and that I should leave by tomorrow.

I drifted through the next few days, complaining to anyone who'd listen about the stubborn crick in my neck, or the fact that one of my eyes hadn't fully opened for weeks, ever since I'd hitchhiked with some Danes across the China–Kyrgyzstan border, riding in the cab of a semi-truck for upwards of thirty hours to arrive, half-blinded, in Osh. No one needed to tell me my piss-poor attitude might ruin the rest of my trip. For a few weeks of June at least, I fully exercised that prerogative.

But even then, with my zeal for travel all but extinguished, I kept working on my project, kept wanting to see a travelogue come together on the page. Thinking about the trip had become its own mania. What would it look like when it was over? What shape would my travels have wrought? A graceful figure eight? A webwork of lines? An ideogram releasing itself from the land? How could I make whatever it was—the totality of this year, its litany of places—clear and communicable to others?

I went into the desert and walked. I needed to start over . . . *Beijing, Wenzhou, Shanghai* . . . to recite the trip from start to finish . . . *Changsha, Guilin, Yangshuo, Guiyang* . . . and bind it all together, itself in itself, with my fragmentary memories of Siberian gulls circling a green lake in . . . *Kunming, Dali, Lijiang, Tiger Leaping Gorge, Shangri-La, Xishuangbanna, Haikou, Sanya, Guangzhou* . . . and the capped kid biking alone down an empty highway, as my own path branched and kept on branching . . . *Kaiping, Shenzhen, Hong Kong, Taipei, Taichung, Sun*

Moon Lake, Manila, Tagaytay, Kuala Lumpur, Kuching . . . and the boatmen jumped down into the water, shoulders bunching against the prow, so we could finally make it . . . *Bako National Park, San Francisco, Hangzhou, Chongqing* . . . to see the joss sticks burning in my mother's hands, the iron cauldrons full of 火 in . . . *Chengdu, Xi'an, Huashan, Qingdao, Tianjin, Dandong* . . . where snow fell into the open plaza of the train station as I looked up from my computer and . . . *Changchun, Changbaishan, Harbin, Heihe, New Delhi, Kathmandu, Chisapani, Nagarkot* . . . all ended, sending my trip down through *Hailar, Hohhot, Yinchuan, Zhongwei, Lanzhou, Jiayuguan, Dunhuang* . . . to meet that Australian couple in the cave carved with flying apsaras, the man inquiring about my project, demanding to know its "focus," which of course had been abstracted by then . . . *Turpan, Ürümqi, Karamay, Hoxtolgay, Kashgar, Tashkurgan, Karakul Lake* . . . dissolved, completely, in the wonder that shines after motion, much like the freight trucks crossing the Karakoram this night are also disappearing around the bend, headed, maybe, for . . . *Osh, Arslanbob, Bishkek, Istanbul* . . . my friend kissing me atop a reggae club called Nayah, the music spinning us away in centrifugal rotations until . . . *Xining, Qinghai Lake, Guide, Tongren, Xiahe, Langmusi, Songpan, Jiuzhaigou, Emei Shan, Wulong, Chishui, Zunyi, Xiamen, Wuyuan, Tunxi, Huangshan, Zhoushan,* were also places that I'd gone, and the last new stroke of eighty . . . *Ningbo* . . . had fallen into place.

I went somewhere. I came back.

THE FIRST WORK OF LITERATURE I REMEMBER BEING ASSIGNED in high school was also a travelogue, a short story called "A Worn Path" by Eudora Welty. In that story, Phoenix Jackson must go to town to buy medicine for her grandchild. Many obstacles appear in Jackson's way, including deep, dark woods, a steeply sloping hill, unforeseen meetings with menacing strangers, a bush that snags on her dress. My teacher chose the story as a lesson in allegory, telling us that the deep, dark woods and the strangers running interference all added up to one symbol: the path Jackson was forced to walk. That path was a metaphor for life itself, and when Phoenix Jackson gets to her path's endpoint, "There I sat and forgot why I made my long trip."

When Bakhtin calls every trip an "extratemporal hiatus," he is also referencing a kind of amnesia. This is a period of the traveler's life in which one thing does not necessarily lead to another, and when even those events that initially feel important or unique are quickly subsumed by a surfeit of others. The traveler has effectively ejected himself from linear time, and as a result, he cannot change, nor execute any purpose. "The hammer of events shatters nothing and forges nothing," Bakhtin writes. "It merely tries the durability of an already finished product. And the product passes the test."

I guess I, too, passed the test, and yet in my case, the initial product was not the same as that which came out. Traveling to so many places in so compressed a time changed me. My trip was the first real thing I ever did with my life, even if what I turned my trip into, the figure a trip makes, was untranslatable, impervious to the word.

When all my grant money had been spent, I returned to Shanghai. I threw away my worn-out shoes and closed my Chinese accounts. On my last day in China, I went to meet J at a bookstore on Nanjing Road. We stood by a pile of discounted Tolstoy books and talked about our next steps. J and his partner had tired of the country and were making inroads on a return to Europe. I was flying from Shanghai to New

York and then taking buses to my parents' house in Tennessee, where I wouldn't even unpack before moving to Arizona for graduate school. Before we said goodbye, we each bought the same map of China, a map that still hangs on my wall today.

My mother, for her part, didn't take any souvenirs with her when she left Shanghai for America in 1988; she needed no such reminders. Her grandmother, the one whose looks had skipped a generation, had just died in the city. Now it was Apo who was instructing Mom to leave one place and join her husband. To go out there, and travel.

Was this the closed loop I'd been looking for all along—my trip abroad ending where hers had begun? What if the figure didn't have to end? Or what if the end was only a temporary stay, a period immediately gainsaid by my next step? According to the orientalist Fenollosa, no truly poetic sentence could ever be finished, "save one which it would take all time to pronounce." I could probably spend forever trying to write this odyssey, this odyssey that has already written me.

Book from the Sky (*Tianshu*), by the conceptual artist Xu Bing, is a text composed from four thousand real-looking Chinese characters that Xu incised onto wooden printing blocks using Song dynasty techniques. None of the words in this book can be defined because Xu made them all up. They are nonsensical figures filling a very real book, one that took the artist years of research and labor to print. Upon its publication, *Tianshu* was derided by some critics as a boyish prank that made a mockery of China's storied literary culture. Those with more of a palate for provocation hailed the piece as a sublime meditation on what it means to mean.

In his own reflections on *Tianshu* and what it may or may not mean, Xu writes, "From 1987 to 1991, what was I like? What did I do? I can only say: a person who spent four years of his life making something that says nothing."

Back in Beijing, at the very start of my trip, I remember watching an elderly man practicing calligraphy on the flagstones of Olympic Park. He was using a broom-sized brush to make each character, placing the strokes in water instead of ink. I couldn't read the characters, but I could tell they were the same, that he was writing the same word over and over. Before each word's last stroke had even been laid, the shape of its sign would already be dissipating, rising into the air as vapor or flowing away in rivulets across the stone.

From 2014 to 2015, what was I like? What did I do? I can only say: I was a person whose life was not the words on the stone, but the water leaking away from them, a message graciously erasing itself.

Running Days

TUCSON, ARIZONA

I'm taking a class called "Interior Journeys" with the writer Fenton Johnson. It's a course on the life of the mind: all the different "practices" writers and clerics employ to transport themselves to an interior place of creativity or solace. We've been reading about Thomas De Quincey's opium habit and Suzuki Roshi sitting zazen. This morning, I run with a line from Haruki Murakami in mind: "All I do is keep running in my own cozy, homemade void, my own nostalgic silence." Inside the void, images form and then disperse: fogged air, falling rain, a full moon nesting among the trees. Each memory hits me like a little tremor, an aftershock of some run left unfinished by the road.

In *The Analects*, Zilu asks Confucius if he may inquire about death, to which the Master replies, "You do not yet understand life—how could you possibly understand death?" I don't presume to understand the life I lead, all these miles I spend running alone with the self, and yet with each day's run, Zilu's question repeats: If this is what it is to live—this restless motion, this silly cantering into the light—then, Master, what is its obverse?

KNOXVILLE, TENNESSEE

Runners are like a cult dedicated to distance, not just miles and kilometers, but the very idea of land unspooling beneath the body, of green swards and wet sand and country roads choked with dust and flowering weeds. Distance as a concept more than a metric, and a feeling more than a concept.

I like to think I joined cross-country in eighth grade because I wanted to know what distance felt like, what miles do to a body. Every autumn for the next five years, I showed up to after-school practices and competed at weekend meets; I hydrated when asked to, stretched my spine like a bow each morning beside my coach's trailer classroom. A poor team player, I slacked off whenever I could, but never got around to quitting. By the end of high school, I was running even during the offseason, my body an odometer steadily counting miles.

TUCSON, ARIZONA

Fenton asks everyone taking the class to choose their own practice— something you can do easily and repetitively—and to continue it for the entire semester. Running is an obvious choice for me; it's an activity I already perform, perhaps because I hardly have to think about it as I do it. But the key thing is to be intentional, Fenton tells us; to not just do something, but to do it in an introspective way. Our chosen practice should ideally also support our writing—the practice that, as students of creative writing, we've come here to master.

I go out to run by the dry riverbed of the Santa Cruz River. Six or seven miles accrete, the minutes hanging salted and warm in the desert air. Waiting to cross the street, I feel Murakami's cozy place buckle and then collapse. An ache often starts small before lengthening down the shaft of a leg, spindling in my toe knuckles, the backs of each heel. I've been doing some version of this all semester: going out on runs, thinking about my running, reading tracts of Chinese philosophy that speak in the declarative about fluidity and the "way." I understand such rituals have more than the usual tinge of "self-help" to them, but I am feeling as open as ever to exhortations from within. I want to help myself be better, at both running and writing, to know with some modicum of clarity why I do the things that I do, and how to be more intentional about them.

In the ancient Taoist text known as the *Nei-yeh*, or "Inward Training," I read the following: "Hold fast to this excellent practice; do not let go of it."

WENZHOU, CHINA

I first ran in China at a track near my paternal grandparents' apartment. I was eighteen and staying with Yeye and Nainai for the summer. They were excited to have me, even if I'd waste much of that summer hiding out in their attic, wondering morosely what my friends were up to back in Tennessee.

I was afraid I'd never see those friends again after fall came and we'd all dispersed to different colleges. (It somehow didn't occur to me that my octogenarian grandparents were an even more temporary presence.) In the attic, which was also my bedroom, I positioned myself right under the air-conditioning unit's sweat-wicking current, daydreaming about chlorinated pool water sluicing down the back of a boy I was already preemptively missing. My grandparents lived right behind one of the city's main trash collection centers. Their apartment was clean, verging on ascetic, but afternoons in that neighborhood still smelled of urban decay.

Every day, I'd go to the track and run two or three miles as my yeye paced around the white-painted perimeter. We were always alone on those days, Yeye comfortably dressed in pajama pants and a flimsy white tank, his grandson bare-chested and red-faced, running. Every day was hotter and more humid than the day that preceded it. Yeye would bring a bottle of water for us, as well as a towel ready to be moistened.

Those sessions at the track return to me now with an eerie clarity. I can still picture the plastic buckets left out for the rain and hear the sound of a game show playing from the gatehouse television. Most of all, I remember Yeye strolling beside the track with his hands behind his back, always moving in the same direction as I, but at a different pace.

TUCSON, ARIZONA

Maybe I run because of vanity, not reverence for distance. I run because American culture values fitness and rewards fit-looking people, because miles keep my stomach tight and my legs slender. There is indeed a self-aggrandizing air to each successful run, and running down a city's main thoroughfare can feel a little, or a lot, like showing off, preening. "Run, Forrest, run!" the driver of a Jeep Cherokee crows.

One of my goals for the semester is to transcend such self-consciousness, to run with no awareness of being watched, and so to pass through the land as a ghost might. I tell myself that no run can be "successful" unless I cross over into this paradoxically active zone of nonexistence, my usually scattered mind wholly surrendered to the present. This is Laozi's area of expertise, not Confucius's—"They do not make a display of themselves and so are illustrious."

Running is one of the best ways I've found to encode a new place into my system. Having mostly learned to run in green, humid places, often beside bodies of running water, I'd assumed that shadeless, waterless Tucson would resist any cultivation of distance. Within a few weeks of moving here for graduate school, however, I was running more than I ever had. I ran mostly in the evenings, when my classes were out and the heat was almost bearable. Repeatedly running a city's streets and byways commits them to muscle memory. On routes I run frequently, like the eight-mile loop from my apartment, up to Grant Road along the Santa Cruz riverway and back, specific landmarks impart a sense of progress, time, and direction. My body starts to know—at this bridge, this cottonwood, this snatched view of "A" Mountain—that it has run four miles, or that an hour has passed, or that it must swerve left to turn a sharp corner. On some runs, like today's, none of these reference points are set, and distance feels like uncertainty. I run south, tentatively, collecting and collating information as I go. These are facts, or really intuitions, about elevation change, shade coverage, traffic density, a run's overall aesthetic appeal. At some point, I stop noticing such details and start to coast, caught unawares by the strangely tender onset of a runner's high. I relax into it, the run; I am dislocated, but pleasurably so, in the newness of my environment, the long underpass near the air force base I experience as a climax.

Back at my apartment, I strip naked and sit on the carpet, reading Thomas Gardner's *Poverty Creek Journal*. I've been told by a fellow runner that this book is like scripture for our secular religion—a trail runner's devotions, amassed over four seasons of runs by a creek in Virginia. Gardner blends reports on his running with gleanings from the poetry of Emily Dickinson and Wallace Stevens, as well as reflections on the death of his younger brother, who was also a runner.

Here in Tucson, I borrow Gardner's structure and adapt it to my practice. I run less than he does, but still, I find it helpful to sit down each Sunday to reflect on the week's mileage, the damage as much as the growth.

KNOXVILLE, TENNESSEE

Each run secretes a route, an invisible line the runner leaves behind in her wake. My mother uses the MapMyRun app to collect digital snapshots of her line drawings. She is the one other person in my family who also likes to run, who gets so worked up about distance. On my birthday each year, she will run exactly 5.29 miles in honor of the date and send me a screenshot after. When one of her children is traveling, she will run 6.66 miles, a number that in Chinese is 六六六—slang for "go smoothly."

I didn't run with my mother when I was still living under my parents' roof. Those were also the years when I technically spent the most time with Yeye and Nainai. They'd come over from China and stay with us for months, cooking our meals and watching me and my siblings when my parents couldn't. Neither of my grandparents spoke English or knew how to operate a vehicle; they rarely left the house and thus were easily evaded. I would often tell them I was going for a run and then disappear for an entire afternoon. They must've thought I was some kind of ultramarathoner in training, and not just a teenage ingrate, trying to get some "distance" from his family.

WENZHOU, CHINA

Every runner has to be okay with inviting distance into their life, with carrying it around and following its commandments. Intimacy for a runner might best be exemplified by those moments of contact that curve away from us on the path. Even when you go jogging in a group, to run is to spend time with other people without really being there, or having to acknowledge, too directly, their company. It's similar, in a way, to growing up in the care of family members you don't know how to relate to, people who are easy to keep pace with but who remain alien to you—and you to them—in almost every way.

In 2014, I moved to China right after finishing college. My mother gave me a package of craisins to deliver to Yeye for his eighty-fifth birthday. "It's his favorite American food," she told me. "Don't forget to save them until you get to Wenzhou." Drunk one night in Beijing, I forgot, and split the bag with a friend.

No one bothered to tell me Yeye was dying until I got to Wenzhou and could see it for myself. He looked painfully thin, and I could hear him struggling to clear his mouth of spit each morning. Once, he went with me to the track to watch me run, but then had to retreat to his bed for the rest of the day, curled into an S-shape on his side.

I had no idea how to help him, though Nainai said just being there was enough. We spent most of each day keeping tabs on him for each other. Yeye napped on and off in the apartment's main bedroom as Nainai sat in the kitchen, mildly manic. I listened to her call Yeye's doctors every day, asking for adjustments to his treatment. Afterward, she would call around to different friends and former students so she could complain about the doctors. Sometimes, at night, while I tried to read James Agee's *A Death in the Family*—a book I now felt queasy about bringing—Nainai would perch on a stool by my bed and talk at me, eventually lapsing into Wenzhounese, a dialect I don't speak. *She just needs to talk*, I told myself, and offered a knowing nod at the more pregnant pauses. I imagined all the stories she was maybe telling me about Yeye's past, the life lessons she was trying to dispense on his behalf, how he would've told me all this himself if he could. 我明白, I kept saying in Mandarin whenever she looked like she needed a response. "I understand."

Some of my extended family came into town for the Mid-Autumn Festival. A cousin of mine who'd undergone some medical training filled me in on Yeye's diagnosis: lung cancer, almost certainly terminal. "Nainai's full of wishful thinking," he said. "Please don't listen to her." I asked him if there was anything we could do—palliatively speaking, that is. "It's incredible, I see Yeye smile every day," my cousin responded, not really answering my question.

When language is confusing or opaque, a family can turn to gestures and acts to abate a feeling of distance. I remember Yeye showing me how to make my bed when I was young. He'd hold two corners of the sheet while I held the others, and then we'd meet in the middle. I remember watching Nainai do the same exercises on our driveway in Tennessee each morning, her dedicated habit of walking back and forth while hitting herself lightly on both arms and legs. In Wenzhou, I ate everything that was set before me, soft slips of banana and pear. I touched Yeye's shoulder when he sat up in bed, and tried to communicate my care and sorrow to him through watchful contact, not words.

"Please take some pictures with your yeye before you leave," my mother told me, and *this* directive I didn't forget. On his birthday, Nainai and I helped him walk to the middle school across the street where both my grandparents used to teach. We asked the guard on duty to take a picture of the three of us standing together at the schoolyard gates. Yeye wore a white short-sleeved shirt and khaki pants. He carried a Panama hat with a black band in case of sun. I'm tempted to quote that Susan Sontag line about every photo being a memento mori, but this photo, for me—it grapples with life, quoting Laozi instead: "Take stock of the family by looking at the family."

That afternoon, I went back out to run. The track felt constraining, so I ran on the paths by the Oujiang River instead, loping past couples walking wispy toy dogs and picking my way down to the docks where all the ferrymen idled. Yeye grew up on the other side of the river, I reminded myself, the other side to which he'd soon return. I ran until the wind's passing flume had set me right, and then I ran back to my grandparents' apartment.

It's closeness as much as separation that matters here. The runner's distance is always a near one.

TUCSON, ARIZONA

Maybe runners are just people trying to be rivers: all that flowing, erosive motion. A few weeks ago, while out on a run, I witnessed the

Santa Cruz actually look like a river. Passing below a bridge that day, I saw brown water gushing over the litter-strewn rocks and coyote scat, reopening a path the river once knew. "All water has a perfect memory and is forever trying to get back to where it was," says Toni Morrison. You run for miles and miles, only to wind up back at your apartment. But slowly, unsurely, a riverbed is changed, a path worn smooth by its runners. The *Nei-yeh* holds that the only way to attain "vital essence" is to condition the body, achieving an ideal alignment of breath and posture. It's a little hokey, I know, but today I run to strengthen my own inner space, to make, of my body, a conduit for the rain.

DALI, CHINA

In the months following my last visit to Yeye and Nainai's apartment, I traveled extensively across China and its neighbors. I wanted to catalog Taoism's "Ten Thousand Things," to revel in transience even as I denied its mortal message—that all things pass, all things die. I traveled a total of 124,274 kilometers that year, a number equal to three equatorial laps around the Earth, eighteen trips down the Nile, forty-three transcontinental drives of the US, or 24,855 high school cross-country meets. Calculated another way, 122,274 kilometers is ten times the distance between Wenzhou, where my Yeye, Nainai, and father grew up, and Knoxville, where I was born, which is to say it is a distance not casually crossed.

On the other side of the country from Wenzhou, I left my bed to run the rice paddies outside of a tourist-filled city. Dogs barked. A sleepy water buffalo pissed into the earth. My path narrowed and raised into a thin bridge that eventually led me to a dramatic coda: an old cement wall, vine-wrapped and crumbling and painted with characters spelling out, in Chinese, "The End."

HAIDA GWAII, CANADA

No cars used this road, so I ran directly on the asphalt, my gait tracking the setting sun, the vanishing road, the linear pleats of cloud above. Caught on a whim, I swerved onto a side path and came up short. There, splayed across my path, the bleached white skeleton of a deer, its face turned toward mine. "We are born from a quiet sleep, and we die to a calm awakening," says Zhuangzi.

TUCSON, ARIZONA

When Yeye dies, I am on campus, reading the *Tao Te Ching*. My mother calls. I cancel my classes and vacuum my apartment before taking my usual run. On this day of all days, I go a considerable distance, not wanting to break my pattern.

A friend drops me off at the airport the next morning. On the plane, I find Delta's marketing lingo more moving than usual: "Because there is no stop in us, or you, only go." Soon I am back in Wenzhou, even if my jet-lagged mind is partly sequestered in Tucson. My father and cousin have come from Tennessee, my brother from Chicago, my uncle and aunt from Hangzhou. All of us, including Nainai, stay at a hotel equidistant to both funeral parlor and cemetery. It's called the 华侨饭店, or "Overseas Chinese Hotel."

The mortuary holds multiple services concurrently, in different halls. We know which hall to go to because a black and white portrait of Yeye sits on an easel outside, garlanded in lilies. Inside, there are more flowers, as well as a small but talented brass band. Each member of the immediate family is given a scrap of paper denoting their relation to Yeye—I pin the word *grandson* and a white carnation to my lapel. We take turns saying goodbye to Yeye from across a moat of flowers (it's not exactly open casket, but there's a plastic panel set into the coffin so we can see his face). Before I can ask "What now?" I'm being pulled into a circle, everyone holding hands and revolving around the casket. And afterward, there is a short eulogy: a student and later colleague of Yeye's says a few words about his qualities as a mentor, his diligence and discretion.

As a family, we line up and shake each departing mourner's hands. Then we follow the band and the pallbearers to the on-site crematorium, where we watch the bearers deposit Yeye's bundled body into an oven and close the door. "I'm not sure they show this part in America," I remark to my brother. We're then led to a small waiting room, where the TV screen streams live footage of the oven—not its insides, thankfully, but its blank metal doors. The immolation goes quickly, and within an hour, we're pulling up to the cemetery. We hike up a terraced hill on the Oujiang's northern bank and place Yeye's ashes in a preselected stone niche, a gray drawer the bricklayers will come that same day to seal. My aunt distributes fake money we shall burn to finance Yeye's next life. We toss these bills into the flames along with each of our paper labels and a cardboard Mercedes. When this is done, we stand with our backs to the river, its turgid length, thinking separately and yet together that we are the ferrymen now.

WENZHOU, CHINA

Many people seem to think running is all about letting go of pain, of desire, of the kinetic energy pent up in a body. For me, a run does the opposite: it helps me retrieve. Like an orb weaver eating its own thread, I return to where I've been: the hills and the back roads, the Arizonan arroyos, that oval track in Wenzhou. Retention is my struggle, not the profligacy of letting go.

Gardner, still mourning his brother, writes near the end of *Poverty Creek Journal*, "What I remember, though, is the hill behind the runner and the sky behind the hill"—images of a perfect distance.

What I remember is fogged air, falling rain, a full moon nesting among the trees. After Yeye's funeral, the jet lag keeps me up. Around one in the morning, I lace on my shoes, exit the hotel, and run back to the Oujiang. I can't say how long I go. My usual landmarks are missing, the river's far side obscured by a dense wall of fog. Many miles later, on a wooden boardwalk by a tree-lined pond, I slow to a jog. The rain has stopped, and the pond water is as dark and shiny as lacquer. A silvery light perfuses the scene, alerting me to an open aperture between worlds, where the stillest possible waters meet air. As usual, a small but profound distance intercedes. At the pond's surface, the trees arc down in a cascade of branches to grasp at their own reflections, trying to touch what isn't there.

TUCSON, ARIZONA

And then, as always, a redux. By the dry river, I run hard and feel the city open up to my stride. The air is clear, my inner void cloudless tonight. This sense of oneness will end. I know that much at least, how every runner's high is let loose and then contained, reeled back into the body's exertions, its annals of loss and inventories of gain. Right now, the balance is held by the path and its white-painted margin. I follow that line, running. I give fealty to the way.

Driving Days

KINGSTON PIKE, TENNESSEE

By June, I'd started putting the pieces in motion. I went to Tennessee to renew my license and borrow my mother's Camry. I fished my old butterfly net out of the closet, bought a tent and a Coleman lamp off Craigslist, sketched out a route in black Sharpie on a AAA map, told some friends I was coming, told other friends I was leaving, told my mother I was "writing," and then drove her car onto the highway. I figured I had a few weeks, maybe less, until this wild inclination to see the country had soured. I wanted to make the feeling count.

US ROUTE 61, MISSISSIPPI

At the Red Carpet Inn outside Natchez, a blond boy who looks too old for his diaper is playing on the stairs. He's holding a toy gun in his hand, which he points at me now like a question: *Bang bang?*

I mime a rebuttal shot from below. The boy smiles. For several minutes, we strafe the night air with invisible bullets, we dodge and we dive, until the boy gets bored and retreats back to his room. Someone swats at a gap in the blinds, someone else returns with a bucketful of ice. I drop my cigarette on the ground and exhale.

INTERSTATE 20, TEXAS

This is the summer of the record-breaking heat; the summer of the Pulse nightclub shootings in Orlando; the summer every gay bar in the South plays "This Is What You Came For" by Rihanna and Calvin Harris; the summer of *Lemonade* and *Captain America: Civil War*; the summer of people in the streets shouting, "Say their names!" (Freddie Gray, Alton Sterling, Philando Castile); the summer people still feel shocked by our American perdition, by drone strikes abroad and mass shootings at home; the summer of all my worst haircuts, and peeing in Starbucks cups while mired in traffic, and slipping a single cigarette behind my ear as I drive because I'm on a break from my MFA and my intentions are artistic.

Outside Abilene, I hear on the radio that carbon dioxide in the atmosphere has reached 400 parts per million—a tipping point, the climate scientist on the line is saying. I set the radio to scan and the chatter refocuses around Pulse, then stocks, then Trump. Every other station is prayer.

I'm not unworried about the state of the world, its warming, all the gas I put in my tank, but still, this particular errand can't wait. This errand is one of retrieval, though the man I'm following has hardly been lost. Over the course of his long life, the writer and lepidopterist Vladimir Nabokov authored more than fifty books in both English and Russian. One of those books, *Lolita* (1958), is now considered a classic American tale of perversion and road travel. Nabokov took to the road almost every summer while writing his opus. Setting off from either Cambridge or Ithaca, he could range as far as the Pacific coast and back in the course of a summer, jotting down notes on five-by-seven-inch index cards as prairie air gusted through a passenger-side window, or holing up for weeks of frenzied writing in a cabin outside Ashland, Oregon, or Afton, Wyoming. When not writing, he'd hunt butterflies in all the public parks and forgotten copses, a passionate pastime he'd taken up as a child.

I first heard about Nabokov's road trips while doing research in a zoological museum at Harvard where he once worked as curator of lepidoptera (moths and butterflies). Many of the insects Nabokov caught on his trans-America road trips were stored in the museum's butterfly room, each specimen affixed to a label listing its Latin name, geographic provenance, date of capture, and collector, V. Nabokov. A framed portrait of the man, taken for *Life* magazine, hung over a table filled with microscopes. In the photo, he's sitting at that same table, staring down his aquiline nose at a butterfly impaled on a pin. I spent much of a long winter hunkering under that gaze, reading Nabokov's memoir *Speak, Memory* as I put the finishing touches on my senior thesis—a study of wing colors in a hyperdiverse clade of butterflies. My sense of time in that place would occasionally fibrillate, quivering in dense pockets of rococo detail that only the microscope's "bright well-hole" could reveal. When not sitting still, I bumbled about the museum of tiny dead things, pulling shards of color from the archives as the campus outside was draped in minimalist white. A faculty reviewer would later rebuke my thesis for hearkening back to a time when scientists still wrote by "quill and ink," a complaint I quickly shrugged off, as it seemed to indicate that some of my other, unmentioned mentor's lessons had stuck.

In the final chapter of *Speak, Memory*, Nabokov likens his life to "a colored spiral in a small ball of glass." This spiral had three distinct sections. Nabokov's childhood in Russia, the "thesis" of his life, forms the spiral's innermost curve, without which nothing else could make sense. This thesis is paired with its antithesis, the spiral's second curve, in which Nabokov's aristocratic family is expelled from Russia and scattered across Western Europe. A later migration, this time to America on the eve of World War II, inaugurates the spiral's third, and presumably final, curve: a time of happy middle age and growing literary acclaim. Nabokov identifies this phase as a "synthesis— and a new thesis." He would never set foot again in the Russia of his youth, but in America he recovered precious reminders of that place, which is to say he found that time, for him, was not always irreversible. Motoring down a roadway in central Colorado or upstate New York, Nabokov was constantly being sent back to a Russia that both used to be and never was, an idyll in the mind that no amount of distance could suppress.

How palpably he missed his roots; how obsessed he was with place. These were the factors that most endeared Nabokov to me as both writer and lepidopterist. By college, feeling vexed by geography already seemed like my default setting. It wasn't just that I felt "out of place" in certain surroundings; it was like my surroundings always demanded a choice—China or America? The South I grew up in or the North where I was educated?—and making such a choice meant giving up part of who I was. In Nabokov, I found someone who bore fierce attachments to both his ancestral home (Russia) and his port of lucky arrival (America), and who was often shuttling between the two in his mind. I nearly shivered when I first came across his declaration that he had to "invent America" before he could write about it, to traverse this nation as both a physical reality and a daunting piece of artifice. "I am driving off to California to-morrow with butterfly-nets, manuscripts and a new set of teeth," Nabokov wrote in 1941 to his friend Edmund Wilson. It was the beginning of his first American road trip. He would see the North Texan plains, the Grand Canyon, the redwood forests near San Francisco. Years later, when asked by an interviewer what memories he held dearest, Nabokov responded, "Meadows. A meadow with Scarce Heath butterflies in North Russia, another with Grinnell's Blue in Southern California. That sort of thing."

My goal this summer is to find "that sort of thing."

SPEEDWAY BOULEVARD, ARIZONA

I stop off in Tucson, where I've been living for about a year. At the University of Arizona's Center for Creative Photography, I look at some photographs by Tseng Kwong Chi. Born in Hong Kong, raised in Canada, educated in Paris, and drawn, like many gay men, to the bright lights of 1980s New York, Chi made a career out of interloping. His photo series *East Meets West*, or the *Expeditionary Series*, documents the many adventures of Chi's alter ego, an Asian diplomat dressed in a Mao suit, sunglasses, and slip-on loafers. Chi photographs himself as this dapper figure before a slew of iconic American backdrops, from Mount Rushmore to the Empire State Building. The cumulative effect of the series is part comedy, part discord—a caricature of Asiatic foreignness spliced into an American hagiography of place. Unknowing viewers might assume they are looking at snapshots of a foreign dignitary's recent press tour. Where has this intrepid

Asian emissary not been? What exactly makes these scenes so American, this portrait sitter so very not?

Looking at Chi's images, I'm struck by the relative sincerity of my own Chinese American family's photo albums, all these pictures of us hamming it up in front of Spaceship Earth or on top of the World Trade Center, my brother and I dressed in the orange-and-white colors of the Tennessee Volunteers as excess SPF dripped down our cheeks. Before they could afford foreign destinations, my parents liked taking the family on road trips all across the Eastern Seaboard. At dawn, we'd leave Knoxville in our white Honda Odyssey to arrive by nightfall at some ticky-tacky motel room whose dimensions and decor never changed in the slightest. We saw the Washington Monument and Niagara Falls in this fashion, Key West's "Southernmost Point" sign and the giant arch vaulting over St. Louis. My father clenched his fist in an almost competitive way every time he beat a yellow light. My mother managed the map.

In every place that we stopped, my parents also put the family point-and-shoot to work, and though I don't believe this documentary impulse is restricted to Asian Americans, such collecting does seem to carry a dual significance for families who moved here from somewhere else. Each picture functions not just as a keepsake, but as an assertion, however offhand, of belonging. We were out here to see America, and to see ourselves amidst it. Still, what I remember best about those road trips are the car rides themselves. The car—its hours of forced proximity—could turn us temporarily into just another American family bent on summertime recreation. Of course, members of this family would sometimes ask, "Are we there yet?" and fight for control of the radio, but in general, car times were good times, times in which our greatest debates pitted Subway against McDonald's, and the whole car's primary aim was getting to one place in a timely fashion, together.

I like to think that Nabokov's road trips were also such prosaic, family affairs. He had his arrogances, but he did not dissemble, did not style himself as explorer or vagabond. He wasn't Sal Paradise in Jack Kerouac's *On the Road*. He wasn't even John Steinbeck in *Travels with Charley*. Nabokov recalled driving a car only twice in his life, and both times he crashed. It was his wife, Vera, who drove the family Oldsmobile down all those Western roads, who changed the flat tires and kept a pistol stowed in her purse. It was also Vera who, in remote lodges and borrowed summer homes, typed out each day's sentences as her husband dictated from across the room. Dmitri, the couple's only son, completed the family trinity. When asked once by a barber where his home was, Dmitri replied that he lived in "little houses by the road."

BIG COTTONWOOD CANYON ROAD, UTAH

My friend Meagan has elected to have her birthday at a yurt high up in the Wasatch Mountains. All our Civics and Suburbans stall halfway up the mountain; only Meagan's Subaru Outback makes it to the top. The woods up here are soggy with meltwater. I catch a brace of day-flying moths and a tiger-striped swallowtail. "Winged clichés," Nabokov would've declared them, lepidopteran platitudes.

When the festivities are over, I drive to Alta, an après-ski town where the Nabokovs summered in 1943. I traipse about, swinging my net, catching a few members of Nabokov's favorite butterfly family, the lycaenid blues. "I have trudged and climbed some 600 miles in the Wasatch Mts and made some superb entomological discoveries. Lovely melmoths and bread-and-butterflies," he wrote to Wilson from Alta. A much lazier "lepist," I keep to the lower trails, where freshly emerged adults, wings still dewy with chrysalis juice, hide out in the columbine and Indian paintbrush. Some fly so slowly I can gather them by hand.

I won't euphemize what happens next: I murder each butterfly for my collection. The fact that I am tapping an abundant and likely renewable resource scarcely betters my position. One can know that to claim an insect life hardly affects its species' prospects, but an execution is still an execution, each killing an intimate act of cruelty.

Like Nabokov, I snuff my butterflies the "Continental" way. I take each insect between two fingers and deliver a short, sharp pinch to its thorax. If I do this with speed and conviction, there is no mess of abdominal breakage, no excess shedding of scales from the wings. Even the most fastidious lepist soon learns, however, that to hold a thing of beauty is to watch it go still in your hands.

MORAINE AVENUE, COLORADO

Meagan joins me for a few days of driving. The Camry hoards our candy wrappers and our gossip. We play "A Sorta Fairytale" by Tori Amos, "Amelia" by Joni Mitchell, and "Fast Car" by Tracy Chapman. Camping outside Telluride, we sleep in a grove of white aspen, each tree an offshoot from the same root system, their collective body known as a "trembling giant." I lend Meagan my copy of *Lolita* to read, telling her that the book ends somewhere in the mountains near where we've staked our tent. That night, it rains so hard that the rain fly on my tent fails to keep us dry. I wake up in the morning to find that the words in my journal have all run together, the mélange of these days.

Stopped over the following night in a town of little glamour, Meagan and I decide it's time to go out. I don a vintage satin bomber jacket printed all over with a map of the world. She pulls on a black velvet dress and pointy pink pumps. We find a bar conveniently located by a Cici's Pizza franchise. We're sitting inside, comparing Kardashians and drinking, when a man in head-to-toe denim comes over to speak with us. I expect him to buy Meagan a drink, but the man's attention is firmly on me. He puts a hand very formally on my back, right over the former USSR, and looks me in the eyes in this queer, searching way. "You let him know if anyone here gives you trouble," he says, nodding to the man behind the bar. Meagan and I say nothing. The man walks out of the bar, and I feel like I'm missing either a punchline or a punch.

Earlier this summer, at a pool party in Atlanta, another man had approached me and a friend to hash out his feelings about Pulse. That man had wanted to understand how such a tragedy—forty-nine mostly Brown and Black men shot and killed in a gay nightclub— could still happen in what he kept calling "my America." This man had his theories, and they all involved blaming the victim. "I just have to ask," he said to us, the two most conspicuously homosexual people at the party, "why is it that y'all need to act like women?" My friend and I were just drunk enough for this shit, so we tag-teamed an intro lecture to Gender Studies 101, explaining to this man that how people perform their gender and who they like to fuck are not necessarily related, that queerness is not just gender inversion, but a complex weave of different sexual practices and identities. By the end of our spiel, we realized we were talking to ourselves.

It feels ungenerous to shove these two men into the same vignette, but both remind me of one of the American road trip's basic tenets: the people you meet are not there to illustrate your ideations of nationhood; they, too, have their own snow globe nations in mind, and sometimes you don't fit into their concept of American rightness when you strut into their local saloon-style bar to order a whiskey pickle back and a veggie burger; sometimes you arrive, in more ways than one, from a place far away that they define themselves against, and sometimes they like the "diversity" you bring and sometimes they don't.

Nabokov didn't try to fit in as he traveled. He'd have Vera sporadically stop the car so that he could trawl the roadsides with his net—let any and all passersby gawk. Though he and Vera were both naturalized in 1945, they rarely defined themselves by such pedestrian yardsticks as party and nation. If anything, Nabokov saw his own autobiography as the silken cord that held his world together. He often wrote of Colorado as a throwback to a Russian childhood he'd already lived. Its alpine glens reminded him of the countryside near Vyra, his mother's estate outside St. Petersburg. In *Speak, Memory*, Nabokov writes of catching, at Vyra, a butterfly of particular beauty that he later lost, "a splendid, pale-yellow creature with black blotches, blue crenels, and a cinnabar eyespot." Forty years later, Nabokov reports recapturing this specimen in America, perched on "an immigrant dandelion under an endemic aspen near Boulder." Both butterfly and man had undergone many displacements since last they met, but their essential identities—the names that go on the label—were still the same.

After dropping Meagan off at the airport, I drive in circles around the Denver suburbs, searching for my own butterfly on its immigrant dandelion. In Estes Park, Colorado, Nabokov once spotted a hawk moth of the genus Celerio, "poised above the water, facing upstream against a swift current, in the act of drinking." That stream now flows past a Starbucks, a Shell, and many different parking lots, but for old times' sake (his times, not mine), I go and stand on a bridge over the water, dead butterflies in my pocket, and turn my face into the current.

AVENUE X, KANSAS

Nabokov finished an early draft of *Lolita* in 1953, while lepping in Portal, Arizona. The book famously recounts a pederast named Humbert Humbert's kidnapping and exploitation of a young girl he calls "Lo." After murdering Lo's mother, he takes the girl on a road trip lasting many months, time enough that the pair "crossed and recrossed the Rockies," experienced "agriculture on a grand scale" in the Midwest, and got to see the dubious sights of "Obvious Arizona." Betwixt and between all these places, in parked cars and on motel bedspreads, Humbert rapes his ward.

"By putting the geography of the United States into motion, I did my best for hours on end to give [Lo] the impression of 'going places,' of rolling on to some definite destination, to some unusual delight." This is the America that Humbert invents for Lolita: a kitschy patchwork ideal for the solicitation of children. Humbert uses the road on Lo like a quaalude, quelling her pained struggles for attention, succor, and, later on, flight. He channels the trip's many sights into a distracting and dissociative mirage, "the whole arrangement opening like a fan, somewhere in Kansas."

In other words, I know to be cautious, to be wary of the landscape and its apparent innocence. And yet, when I'm out here, driving, the sky and the grass and that distant line of hills can sometimes amalgamate in a way that chases gasps of wonder out of me. I pull over whenever this happens, genuinely concerned I might crash; I watch the clouds skate through the lower atmosphere. If I'm lucky, their bubbly tops will intercede between me and the sun, chiseling the light into lambent shafts called "crepuscular rays" that I, in my atheist irony, like to think of as the "God light."

LOCUST STREET, KANSAS

On those rare occasions when Nabokov traveled to give lectures while Vera stayed at home, she was his favorite correspondent. To her, he wrote treacly, confiding letters that spared no detail of his days. Often, he'd enclose a freshly caught butterfly with each letter, its body stashed in its own waxy, glassine envelope.

Though I don't have any partner waiting at home, I too have been compiling, via Grindr, my own bodily impressions of Americana. In Odessa, Texas, weeks earlier, a local guy squired me around his former high school's football stadium, where we sat in the stands, looking for Mars. By Denver, my liaisons had grown older and far less cagey. They'd catch on quickly when I started complaining about the yoga mat I'd been sleeping on for three days, letting me crash in their four-poster beds after a desultory round of oral. Tonight, I'm hanging out with Tom from Nebraska at a house he's trying to flip, drinking boxed wine and petting a Jack Russell terrier named Sushi. When we get to the kissing part, Tom keeps on talking about the house and its foundations, how very sturdy they are, how in another life, he would've loved to stay, but you know how it goes: student debt, car payments, a mortgage he can't afford. Tom works at an alternative medicine center, administering acupuncture and Reiki. He moved to Kansas City after an abusive two-year relationship with the Castro. I let him say various quasi-racial but ultimately stimulating things to me ("I love how smooth you are!"), and then Tom from Nebraska lies on top of me like a fuzzy, weighted blanket. Afterward, he asks me what I'm doing out here, and so I tell him I'm on a quest for my great white Russo-American daddy. He laughs and says, "Same."

UNNAMED ROAD, NEBRASKA

Deep in the sandhills, a phalanx of dragonflies emerges, dripping, from a lake. Each new adult boasts chartreuse eyes and a lurid orange paint job. There is something cyborgian about them, the metallic sheen of their carapaces, the precise joining of all their parts. Not unlike a car on the road, a dragonfly in motion is carbon fuel and hunger shoved into a chassis, except driver and vehicle are inseparable in this case, the radio's static elaborated into a sibilant voice. That sound hangs over me this evening, a pleasant, enfolding thrum. A few individuals alight on my chest to dry their wings. When they are ready, they lift off my bare skin and start to rise, joining the lake's vast exhalation of matter. For almost an hour, this interspecies catch and release keeps happening to me, and when it's over, I'm lying there in the reeds, reading Hanya Yanagihara's *A Little Life*, and summer still reigns in America.

EAST RAINBOW AVENUE, WYOMING

In Laramie, I locate Matthew Shepard's memorial bench on the local college campus. I sit there with his name at my back and gaze stupidly at my feet. According to an article on the National Park Service's website, "This quiet tribute to a single individual connects his story to the landscape, to his community, and to America's queer cultural legacy."

Our country may be grounded in the land, but what ties places as disparate as Guam and Iowa together, and then us to those places, is inarguably also a concept, an abstraction many of us treat as sacrosanct. Spending hours on the road of this confounding idea, mulling it over, pondering *my America*, is what the standard road trip narrative is all about. Or that's the idea, at least; that's what's supposed to happen. I left on this trip with Nabokov as my lodestar, but a reimagined America my not-so-secret aim. Though I've gone a respectable distance at this point, I still feel like I haven't captured that ineffable Americanness just yet; or maybe I have and don't want to admit it, for the country I've come to know on the road is not a pleasing procession of iconic places, but a chaotic scrawl of ailing infrastructure, of speed traps and exit signs and long-overdue roadwork. These highways and roadsides, a country that literally passes you by, are the only American landscape I feel more connected to now than when I began.

US ROUTE 287, WYOMING

I drive and keep on driving. Saratoga, then Rawlins, then Lander. Outside Dubois, a forest fire has blocked the main route to Teton, so I make camp and look for an alternate route. A bearded ex-cop on a neighboring site comes over to ask for a cig and to tell me that the "hotshot wildland firefighters"—they are actually called this—will be here by morning.

Outside the town grocer, a couple on a bike trip strikes up a conversation. The man wants to help me quit smoking. He shows me a picture of a baby on his phone. "That's my great-grandnephew," he says. "I wouldn't have that if I hadn't quit when I was twenty-three." The woman nods amen, then tells me, apropos my face, that her brother used to rent warehouses in the eighties to a Chinese family in Oakland. The matriarch of that family died from cancer. Her widower didn't know any English, and so the teenage son had to step in as the business's de facto boss. "It was so sad, how hard that boy had to work, every morning until every night," the woman tells me. I reciprocate her smile.

GRAND LOOP ROAD, WYOMING

Almost a decade ago, my parents took us on one last family road trip. The tour lasted only two states, but they were the big, square ones out West. We drove all the way from Boulder to Yellowstone, where we spent a frigid morning in the rental car, passing a pair of binoculars back and forth so everyone could say they'd seen an elk. As usual, we only ate dinner at Chinese restaurants, dining in the company of other Asian families on similar trips (no party would acknowledge the others, but still, it was like we'd planned our itineraries together). I remember standing outside one Chinese restaurant in Wyoming, or maybe Montana, waiting for my parents to settle the bill as I tongued my way through a complimentary Life Saver. Cars in the street were slowing down and lowering their windows. After a while, it dawned on me that the pronghorns across the road were real, and that they were looking at me.

That was the America my parents put in motion for me, a space where our Chinese habits of mind and stomach could comfortably mix with Wild West "ghost towns" and the other relics left behind by Manifest Destiny. I realize now that I might have located a more coherent version of my America if I'd directed this trip down that same, yellow-dashed road. Rather than hewing to Nabokov's path, I could've driven around in search of Asian America. I could've signed up for food tours of every Koreatown and Little Tokyo on the West Coast, or spent a few weeks learning about the Hmong diaspora in St. Paul. I could've made pilgrimages to sites of historical significance for East Asians like me: Angel Island, Promontory Point, UC Berkeley and San Francisco State, where Asian American Studies got its start. The main reason I didn't take that trip was because I thought I knew how it ended, with the Asian American man learning how to call these lonely highways and stolen lands his own. This kind of ending rankles me for many reasons, none of which are easy to articulate. It's not that I'm unmoved by all the American Dream's ethnic pleats, but defining myself as a proud Asian American still feels like I'm invoking a simulacrum of this country, one that has been politically and emotionally useful for so many, but which has also created its fair share of internal contradictions and strife. This has been said before, but should be said again: Asians in this country are not all alike; we, too, are imaginary citizens living in imagined community with each another. Some of us have been here longer than others; some of us have more access to Ivy League colleges, boba tea, and cultural capital. Many of us don't know what it even means to be Asian or American, let alone an admixture of both.

To be fair, my parents also never began any of my childhood road trips looking for a distinctly Asian America. (We were driving to the Florida panhandle, not querying our identity.) If they found such a place at all, they found it accidentally, and with pleasure, the Odyssey making an immediate beeline for any Chinese buffet by the highway.

The road of my own choosing dead-ends now at a T-junction outside of Yellowstone. To my east is Heart Mountain, where thousands of Japanese Americans were incarcerated during World War II. To the west, a trio of pronghorns, grazing on a low hill. The beasts, escapees from memory, turn their white hindquarters to me: a slow and graceful mooning.

SOUTH FOURTH OF JULY CREEK ROAD, IDAHO

Up on the Continental Divide, a hailstorm takes me off the road. I set up camp by a lake near Coeur d'Alene and wonder if the time has come to turn back. After almost ten thousand miles, I have tired not of the road, but of driving it by myself.

Karen Shimakawa writes that Asian Americans have always existed as a "frontier" and a "limit case" to American identity. For Shimakawa, this is what makes Asian Americans who we are, this state of simultaneous inclusion and exclusion. We are the model minorities who somehow never made it ashore; the upstanding business owners and academics whose loyalty still can't pass muster; the bougiest ethnic food group, but also the exotic delicacy stuck in America's craw. I want to know how we get past this impasse between alienation and belonging, or if such a stable, unchanging relationship to America is really the endgame we're after. When the hailstorm is over, crushed ice sparkles from the grass outside my tent, and for the rest of the day, my magpie heart is light.

In his *Expeditionary Series*, Tseng Kwong Chi goes from urban sightseer to frontier explorer in the span of a frame. The viewer sees Chi bending at the waist in a Tennessee cotton field, shrunk to lilliputian proportions by Monument Valley. These images evoke the tradition of American landscape photography without conforming to its mold. They possess the grandiose scale and formal austerity you might expect, but stop short of portraying the land as blank and unpeopled, as if the camera lacked an operator. Chi, the queer in the Mao suit, is always there: a yellow man mucking up the white man's dream of an endless, Western Arcadia. My favorite shot shows him standing inside an empty field in North Dakota, a jag of lightning on the horizon and a halo of ozone about his head. Silver light beams from his sunglasses. He has landed in this Ansel Adams–approved scene like some ambassador of the strange, scrambling our lines of sight so that all claims to belonging are suspect. A laminated badge is clipped to his jacket. Sometimes it reads *Slut for Art*, and sometimes it reads *Visitor*.

NE KILLINGSWORTH STREET, OREGON

A friend in Portland invites me to stay for a while, so I do. We sit in the leafy backyards of borrowed houses, ashing into seashells and dodging shrapnel from the squirrel wars raging above. We go out drinking each night and spend the next day hungover in some riverside park where they're playing "Dreams" by Fleetwood Mac and the vibe is all chicken wings and politics.

Nabokov rarely took to any soapbox if he could help it. He would share his strong opinions about writing, other authors, and even lepidoptery with anyone who would listen, but politics—how large groups of people get on with each other—was not one of his favorite topics. In Nabokov's exquisitely tuned prose, issues of historical or social import tend to get lost in what Humbert Humbert might call a "vapory accumulation of sounds." This was part of the point for Nabokov. He wrote in service of an aesthetic experience that elevated life above the profane, that exuded an aura of the everlasting, and that could never be reduced to an argument one might lob at a public debate. The author figure, for Nabokov, was first and foremost an individualist, an artist engrossed in the tracing of his own personal "match themes." Even if events of a political nature had played a decisive role in making the artist who he was, the language of politics was ink for inferior pens. Such language was at once too broad and too partisan, too populous with winged cliché. I may never stop holding my own little torch to Nabokov's notion of art for art's sake, but I also don't want to give up my membership in a collective, or to pin myself, insect-like, to the coattails of one man.

All summer, I've been riding his colored spiral, collecting butterflies in the places he left on his labels, trying to figure out which "match themes" are his and which are mine. I've tried to keep my rhythms simple: each dawn, a cigarette; each dusk, the same. I like sitting there behind the wheel with no destination yet, no book and no net, just watching the sun extend its ligatures of light. All summer, I've also listened for the coyotes that yip across the tracks, seen the worker bees organizing by the apiary, let all the harvestmen and potato beetles come tippling to my rain fly at night. I've kept pitching my little houses by the road—a stake in all four corners, a bundle of firewood as ballast, the best foundations I can make. I always set my tent down as close as I can to the sound of running water. It cuts beneath you, washing up through the floorboards of your dreams, a sound like letting go.

US ROUTE 101, CALIFORNIA

When I finally get to the Pacific, I decide to spring for an Airbnb hosted by a young couple from China. Their wooden house in Crescent City looks nothing like the brick McMansion I grew up in, but it has the same smell, all that ginger and charred rice, and the same basic condiments in the pantry. After I drive away, the couple leaves me a review: "Dai is a very sonny boy, he himself is driving along the coast of Pacific Ocean, this is a lang road. He must be get success on his way of live."

For the time being, I guess I'll stay my course. The ocean turns over slowly in its basin, and everything on this darkening road looks coated in an ethereal medium—my headlights, those stars, his words haunting every turn. I'm getting off the colored spiral soon, the rotary, the traffic circle, whatever you want to call it. I've brought back no souvenirs but these butterflies, the ones drying on my dash. Now that I have them sorted into their little envelopes, I want to send one to everyone I love, each a postcard from my own invented America.

Humbert wonders near the end of *Lolita* about "the secret of durable pigments," a detail that Nabokov leaves unexplained. My guess is that he is alluding here to the structural colors of certain butterflies, those blue, green, purple, or iridescent colors that are produced by a wing's nanostructures and how they scatter or bend the light. Because the chitinous shapes of a butterfly's wing scales are much hardier than any chemical hue, structural colors do not fade in the same way that pigments do. If properly preserved, butterflies blessed with such immutable colors can dazzle for years after their death. That was the goal for Nabokov: a hue that wouldn't run, a pattern irreducible to any other. By most measures, he achieved what he set out to do. How else could I have followed him all this way, or spent all these hours emulating the swish of his net? How else but a legacy, and one more durable than most?

It is within the biography of his most famous character, though, that I find clues to how most of us, good or evil, seem to live our lives. Humbert Humbert's path yields no final, summative conclusion, nor even an appropriate punishment for his crimes. Instead, it ends with our antihero driving on the wrong side of the road somewhere in Colorado. He has no more options, no more places to go. All the dead ends foreshadowed by his choices are converging to meet him, but with them comes this curious, enervating calm.

"Gently, dreamily, not exceeding twenty miles an hour, I drove on that queer mirror side."

A Borderlands Transect

A transect is a line that a researcher, usually a biologist, moves along, collecting data on a place. Transects may span only a few hundred feet or stretch across several thousand miles, in which case they may be conducted by horseback or car. Usually, though, a person walks a transect; a study proceeds step by step.

Back when I was in training to be a biologist, I took a course on ecological sampling. One thing I learned was how to run a transect. My classmates and I were sent into the Australian Outback with lengths of cordage and a white plastic frame known as a quadrat that we dropped on the ground every six feet—in each white box, a pixel of ecology to be analyzed. Our instructors told us to walk the transect slowly, carefully counting up every desert shrub and tuft of grass that fell under the quadrat's purview, and to try and notice how the environment changed as we moved up and down the line. Scientists often use transects to track the population dynamics of endangered animals and plants. They are a method, that is, of gauging abundance. In principle, however, a researcher may use a transect to explore all manner of topics, including incorporeal and esoteric ones. Here, the minimalism of a praxis becomes its strength. Holding a notebook and pen, you chart a path and you walk it, looking for answers to your questions.

I lived in Tucson, Arizona, from 2015 till 2017—the length of time I needed to walk a transect, and to complete an MFA in creative writing. I found that I liked Tucson, but did not get it as a place—not its people nor its environment, not anything about it. When I was there, I felt like a bead of water skating across a hot metal surface. What were these gridded streets unwarped by topographic disturbance? Why did none of the rivers marked on the map resemble proper bodies of water? Who were these "snowbirds," and was I one of their number?

Sometimes, a transect line can begin before the transector even knows what question they're asking. Mine starts from above, with a black plain in an oval window, a black plain just barely sketched with electric light—an image either terribly inauspicious, or obstinately hopeful.

My first week in Tucson, a woman in my program lends me her place to crash as I search for my own apartment (she is off to Tijuana to write a story about something called a zonkey). I have never met this woman before and am touched by her open-door policy to strangers. She is one year ahead of me in the program, a travel writer with several publications already to her name. I have never actually met a writer who wasn't also a professor, let alone lived inside their empty nest, and so I take careful note of the items in this woman's apartment: a bed, a floor lamp, a bottle of Mrs. Meyer's hand soap, a desk stacked with books and marked-up printouts of essays. I have always felt more accomplished at copying other people's aesthetics than creating my own.

I move into an apartment building a few blocks south of campus called the Alamo. The Alamo's main selling point, for me, is the pool in the courtyard. I never get to swim in the pool, as my property manager has it drained and filled in not long after I move in. Eventually, a picnic table is installed on top of what used to be the pool. I think the idea is for the table to create a gathering space for me and my fellow tenants, but there is no shade by the picnic table, and so we all sit on little stools or folding chairs outside our own apartments instead, smoking or scrolling through our phones. Two train lines—one for Amtrak's Sunset Limited and another running north from the border—converge near my apartment. I don't really mind the occasional noise, even when the train cars pass at night. To my easterner ears, speeding trains just sound like the West.

I have implied that I am moving along this transect without a clear question in mind. In reality, I have too many questions, each the basis for some essay I am trying to write and turn in to workshop. The problem is one of focus; I can't keep track of my questions, even though several of them have grown into large, lumbering beasts. I would like to know, for one, what it means to occupy the position that I do—Asian, queer, and likely temporary—within the US–Mexico borderlands, what it means to live and abide here, where so many edge spaces collide. But this is a life question as much as a writing one, which means workshopping can only help so much; it is a question to be asked outside.

My new friend Erika writes in her bio that she used to eat moths as a child. I also like collecting insects, though not often for consumption. I bike over to Erika's house to find her roller-skating on the hardwood, a tumbler of whiskey in her hand. She tells me about CAConrad and Emily Dickinson—the patron poetesses of her bookshelf. "It's kind of scary, but I think she likes me," I tell an old friend who often calls me to compare microtraumas. My friend sighs. "Why do you care so much about being liked?"

Gloria Anzaldúa writes, in her bilingual, hybrid work of poetry and theory *Borderlands/La Frontera*, "A borderland is a vague and undetermined place created by the emotional residue of an unnatural boundary." She writes, further, that "being a writer feels very much like being a Chicana, or being queer—a lot of squirming, coming up against all sorts of walls." One day, I look up to find a tuba-shaped cloud, pinkish and translucent, hovering over the parking lot outside of Walmart, a cloud that Erika decides is more of a pregnant seahorse shape than a tuba. "Did you know that male seahorses are the pregnant ones?" I ask her.

Transectors pose simple questions that aren't always simple to answer. A researcher would like to know, for instance, the number of green figeater beetles (*Cotinis mutabilis*) present on the University of Arizona's main quad. They chart a transect line across campus and walk it, tallying each beetle they spot. The number of beetles observed along the transect is then plugged into an equation that, should certain assumptions be met, provides an accurate estimate of figeater beetle numbers in the entire area of study. One of the assumptions made by this equation is that every object or specimen of interest along a transect line is actually detected by the transector, and that the object or specimen of interest is not confused with something else.

Figeater beetles are endemic to the US–Mexico borderlands. They are often mistaken, perhaps because of their glistening green elytra, for the Japanese beetle (*Popillia japonica*), a notorious invasive from Asia.

"Why am I here?" I ask of the transect. Maybe Tucson could be anywhere, anywhere with low rent and an MFA program. The borderlands, too, might also be transposable. That is to say, what we think of as the borderlands is not just a geographic region straddling two nations, but a set of representations and relations implanted within multiple cultural imaginaries. For Anzaldúa, these more intangible borderlands, which she variously labels as "psychological," "sexual," and "spiritual," are not exclusive to the Southwest. She writes that "the Borderlands are physically present wherever two or more cultures edge each other, where people of different races occupy the same territory, where under, lower, middle and upper classes touch, where the space between two individuals shrinks with intimacy."

"Are you ready to be good friends?" The first question that Erika ever poses to me.

And yet, locality matters—to be in *this* place, moving along *this* transect. I walk in the desert just west of Gates Pass. On the ground, I spot two grayish carabid beetles, as well as a spiny lizard already desiccated into a pseudo-fossil. I take the lizard back to my apartment and store it in one of the plastic Talenti jars in my freezer, which are already full of figeater beetles. I am surprised, again, by the bounty of this environment.

Perhaps a more appropriate question than "Why am I here?" is "Should I be here, incrementally raising the rent?" The writer Leslie Marmon Silko, who has lived outside of Tucson for decades, reported feeling a similar anxiety about belonging when she first moved here in the seventies. Silko grew up on the ancestral lands of the Laguna Pueblo in the American state of New Mexico. Tucson was not located on those lands, and so Silko didn't know if she could ever feel justifiably at home in Tucson. "I used to think there were exact boundaries that constituted the 'homeland,'" she writes, "because I grew up in an age of invisible lines designating ownership." One such invisible line divided Silko from southern Arizona, a largely psychic line that she would do her best to circumvent.

To say that borders like the US–Mexico borderline are false impositions upon a borderless landscape is not to imply that territories and homelands don't exist, or that these entities don't also have edges that rub up, frictionally, against each other. "In Tucson I was not so far from Laguna," Silko observes—an expression of how all earthly places are, in the end, contiguous with all others. But Silko makes this claim humbly, careful to point out that other Tucsonans have connections to this place that antedate hers: "I was in Yaqui country."

I am in Tohono O'odham county as well as Yaqui country. I will not pretend I yet know what this means.

On the bus, I streak north on I-10, heading to visit a friend in Phoenix. A man named Marvin sits down next to me and starts to talk. Marvin has just been released on good behavior after five years in prison (I do not ask about his charge). He tells me he ate something bad in prison, and they'd cut him open to fix it, but now he's been carrying around a hernia for a year. His plan is to go to the Indian hospital in Phoenix to get the hernia fixed. "There were three people who looked like you in there," Marvin says to me. "They stayed with the Chicanos mostly. One of them, I forget his name, fixed my TV for me. He was damn good at fixing things."

Marvin asks if he can borrow my cell phone. I watch his fingers pick at the virtual keyboard and repress the desire to type on his behalf. Later, I will read his texts to an unknown interlocutor, all of which have gone unanswered: "Hey, this is Marvin. I borrowed this Chinese kid's phone." "I'm coming home." "Did you miss me?" "Is there food?" Marvin gets off the bus at Mesa, and I do not see him again.

Much later, I receive a few texts that are meant for Marvin. I quickly respond, telling the person on the other end that I don't know where Marvin has gone, but that he should be coming home shortly. A few minutes go by. Then, another message: "Has he been drinking?"

"What are you writing?" Marvin asked me on the bus. "A letter to a poet," I told him. In one of my classes, the professor had assigned us the following prompt: Write a Thanksgiving letter to a writer you're grateful for. I'd chosen C. D. Wright. "What does she write about?" Marvin wanted to know. "A bit of everything," I said. "Race, justice, and like trying to responsibly be from a place." "Shit," he said. "I could write a book about that."

I don't know if I should be here, and yet I am. After my last workshop of the semester, I write down the following unattributed writing advice: "No one wants to read an apology for privilege." I tend to nod along to this advice, while also wondering why so much writing about privilege is still out there, and why I am often the one reading it. A person walking a transect must ask questions about the area he is crossing, but he must also question the person walking the transect. Who is this person, this supposedly impartial observer? What are his blind spots, his tells, the aspects of the environment, or himself, that cause him to turn away?

As far as writing (and living) advice goes, I far prefer what Raquel Gutiérrez, a writer I met in my program, has to say: "If there was anything to do with your privilege, it was to risk it. And it would never be enough."

One semester ends. C. D. Wright dies of a blood clot that travels to her heart.

By spring, I believe I am noticing more, like how the rubber sleeves of my bike handles leave behind dark thumbprints on whitewashed walls; or how sun spiders differ from scorpions, which differ from the friendly tarantulas housed at the Desert Museum; or how Southwestern sightlines lack both the haze of urban China and the tree cover of the East Coast that I'm used to, and that this brightness, this clarity, can sometimes operate like a barrier. Out in the desert, I can see so far if I find the right vantage, so far that even nearby objects and people start to look distant.

My friend Bonnie visits for a few days. I drive her out to a vast lake bed near Wilcox where the relentless beat of the sun has left behind a powdery white scrim of salt-spackled crane feathers in lieu of water. The two of us walk on the lake bed, looking out at an asymptotic horizon. Metallic-green tiger beetles scout for prey as we advance. (Why is it, I wonder, that all insects in this desert look like emeralds?) According to *An Introduction to Ecological Sampling,* edited by Bryan F. J. Manly and Jorge A. Navarro, transect studies are also referred to as "distance sampling." Across longer transects, the editors admit, errors in sampling are likely to occur—objects miscounted, or totally ignored. "Because of observer bias and other problems," they write, "the assumption of 100% detection of items on the transect line might not be reasonable." To correct for this bias, it's useful to "double observers for some or all of the [transect]." One line with multiple minders.

Back at the Alamo, Bonnie and I sit on the carpet, eating pasta. I start ranting to her about Operation Streamline, a federal policy I've just learned about. Per this policy, migrants apprehended in the borderlands are rapidly prosecuted, tried (sometimes dozens at a time) in a kangaroo court, and then sentenced to prison before being deported. "Most of the prisons are for-profit institutions subsidized by *our* taxes!" I exclaim. Bonnie wants to know if I've "seen" the border yet. I'm confused by this question. I realize I'm not sure what there is at the border to see. In my mind, the border is a wall, or maybe some kind of red line blazed into the dirt, with *us* scrawled on one side and *them* on the other.

I eventually learn that the first people to "see" the border were also the people who set it. In 1848, Mexico and the US signed a treaty of "Peace, Friendship, Limits, and Settlement," thus ceding more than half of Mexico's territory to the victorious Americans. One

year later, teams dispatched by both governments started surveying the new border, which stretched from just south of San Diego
to the mouth of the Rio Grande. A borderline had been agreed
upon but not physically established, delimited but not yet marked.
Surveying the heretofore invisible line took six years in total. During that span, Mexican and American surveyors carefully checked
each other's work, oftentimes disagreeing about where the line was
sited. These disputes continued even after the fifty-four borderland
maps generated by the surveyors were signed by representatives of
both countries in 1857, averring that "these maps and views shall
be regarded as the true line, from which there shall be no appeal
or departure." Controversy over the "true line" spurred a second
binational survey between 1891 and 1894, at which time 258 phallic monuments were installed along the border. The monuments
look like obelisks and are made of iron with a concrete base. They
substantiate a line that previously wasn't there and that, in fact,
doesn't exist.

When the new semester begins, there are parties all the time—
birthday parties and housewarming parties and MFA readings that
turn into parties after a few poems have been read. At these parties,
people sit everywhere. They sit on the floor with their backs against the
oven, on sofas, on the kitchen counter so they can flirt at eye level with
their crush, or outside under the palo verde and citrus trees, smoking
cigarettes and vaping, or else enjoying the secondhand smoke. I strike
up a friendship with another Asian in my program named Kelsey—a
writer of stories our classmates have classified as "speculative." Soon, it
feels unnatural to sit outside any party, smoking any cigarette, unless
Kelsey is inhaling the spirit's other half.

In all honesty, I didn't clock Kelsey as Asian when I first met her, partially because she didn't look like most of the Asians I know, and partially because I didn't expect to meet many Asians in Arizona. Kelsey's father is white, and her mother is Japanese. When Kelsey gets tan, she is what I would call "ethnically ambiguous." My dynamic with Kelsey feels different to my relationship with my other Asian friends, around whom I am always subtly aware of our phenotypic likeness. I feel very close to Kelsey, but part of that closeness is our difference. When we go to shows with Erika, or bike together to Shot in the Dark, the twenty-four-hour café where we write, I do not think we appear, to others, like "those Asians," and yet there is a certain consonance, too, a way that our respective bone structures and hairlines (in Tucson, we both sport undercuts of varying lengths) connect the dots of our race. Once, at the club beneath Hotel Congress, a white woman asks us if we are siblings, a question I at first take as a compliment—like thank you, white woman, for sensing the force field of our closeness. Granted, this woman is also very drunk, and as she kneels on the ground, touching our legs, she says she'd personally like to eat us. No, thank you, we both say, side-eyeing the other.

To live in the borderlands is to continually notice such things: the gradations of difference that hold communities, institutions, and even friendships simultaneously together and at odds. The word *borderlands* is 边地 in Chinese. 地 is a common word for "earth" or "land." According to David Der-Wei Wang, 边 is a versatile word that, as a verb, can apply "equally to the acts of bringing close and setting apart."

I have not seen the border yet, or whatever there is at the border to see, but I think I'm starting to observe this unnatural boundary's effects—the gravity exerted by an invisible line made stubbornly solid.

Like a border, a transect starts as an imaginary line. Transects are often manifested by a rope or a long piece of measuring tape; borders are fortified by phallic monuments, by walls. A researcher walking a transect should ask specific, answerable questions. When a surveyor or border patrol officer "walks the line," they are also asking a question. That question is most often "Who owns this land?" or, relatedly, "Who belongs here, and who doesn't?"

In the decades immediately following the modern border's establishment in 1848, this imaginary line was not guarded. Mexican nationals and Native Americans frequently crossed and recrossed the border for economic purposes or to seek kin on the other side. Few to none of these crossings were curtailed or even monitored. It wasn't until Congress passed the Chinese Exclusion Act of 1882 that the concept of illegal immigration—and, relatedly, a class of people known as "illegal aliens"—entered public discourse. Chinese migrants hoping to find work in the US now had to exploit legal loopholes to enter, or else do so surreptitiously via the northern or southern border. Many of these migrants would book passage from China to San Francisco, where they'd then transfer onto merchant ships bound for ports in northern Mexico. From there, Mexican guides used a variety of tactics to smuggle the migrants across the border, from having them pose as fishermen to leading them across by foot.

The unguarded border was still a gauntlet to be endured, though— Chinese border crossers frequently became disoriented in the desert, and occasionally perished, as one fourteen-year-old boy did, in 1890, from exposure. Many attempts ended in failure, such as the case of a man named Law Ngim, who, after being caught at the border, tried to plead ignorance, saying, "I knew that I didn't have the privilege of entering the United States, but I didn't know I was *in* the United States."

Whether they knew it or not, thousands of Chinese, mostly men, managed to cross America's border during the exclusion era. It would not be inaccurate, as the historian Erika Lee argues, to call these men America's first illegal immigrants, and to name the border-obsessed American nation-state that emerged in response a country premised on "gatekeeping." To the white American public of the late nineteenth century, the ongoing influx of diseased, undemocratic, and sexually immoral Chinese laborers—in direct defiance of federal law, no less—indicated a migrant crisis at the border. This "Chinese Leak," as an article in *Harper's* put it, needed to be plugged. Just as the migrants depended on a multiracial relay team of guides and accomplices to help them cross the border, the US government now tapped into a network of consular officials in Mexico, as well as Mexican and Native informants, to keep tabs on the movements of Chinese migrants in the borderlands and to send pictures of potential crossers to immigration inspectors based in Tucson.

Something else I didn't know before I came here: it was the xenophobic uproar over Chinese immigration during the exclusion years that led to the founding of a department within immigration services dedicated to physically protecting the border. (Officers of this so-called "Chinese Division" were the precursors to today's Border Patrol.) What had begun as a mostly invisible line postulated by treaties now became, for some people at least, a partition.

I walk into the nighttime desert, and Kelsey walks beside me. Our headlamps spotlight the foundations of an abandoned ranch house built in the 1930s, not long after the Border Patrol was officially founded. We help each other climb up onto one of the house's stone walls, turn off our headlamps, and watch the moonlight silver the landscape. I am trying to imagine what it was like for those Chinese migrants who years ago braved this desert, or for those other migrants—mostly from Central and South America, but also Haiti and the Middle East—still currently crossing. I cannot imagine one step from any one of their journeys, and maybe it is not my place to imagine. The migrants out there are walking a similar terrain as I am, just tied to a different line. Another piece of writing advice: trace the connections, but always attend to where they stop.

On the night Trump is elected, my friends and I take shrooms and watch CNN. Artichokes steam on the stovetop as footage of a crowd in Ohio screaming, "Build the wall!" plays across our laptops. After Pennsylvania goes red, the hostess of the party I'm at decides she's going to be sick. She runs a bath for herself as another friend gets up to leave, saying, "Right now, I have to be with my cat."

Kelsey and I bike over to Shot in the Dark. We stand outside the café, admiring our favorite Tucson landmark: a construction crane trellised in Christmas lights. Somewhere down the street, a Jeep full of students waving American flags is beginning a victory lap. Kelsey and I look up at the crane, whose lights tonight shine green. If this had been a regular night, we would've been here, working on our writing, and if what had followed was a regular morning, we would've split a post-writing cigarette beneath the crane, our shared smoke climbing the metal lattice.

But tonight is not every night, and the weeks and months that follow are also, phenomenologically speaking, irregular. A week passes. I turn to Kelsey inside Shot in the Dark and ask, half-joking, if maybe we're still tripping, and maybe if we could just get a little rest, the changes would stop accruing. Yet no one around us is too interested, right then, in getting a little rest. "Every increment of consciousness, every step forward is a *travesía*, a crossing," writes Anzaldúa. Her words become the mantra to my weeks.

That time I ask a friend if she wants to go with me to an informal group discussion about the election. "Liberal circle jerk," she texts back. "But there's food," I respond.

That time another friend, a Trump voter, texts me from Florida to say, "I told you so." When I start to take this a little personally, he tells me to calm down, writing that Trump's election won't be the "end of the world," to which I dramatically respond, "For you, at least."

That time the redheaded woman at the bar keeps saying, "I believe in crystals, I believe in astrology, I believe in reincarnation, I believe."

That time I go with Kelsey to buy more psychedelics from a sixteen-year-old dealer who asks us to call her Elvis.

That time people on social media are recommending we reread *Harry Potter*, or sign all the petitions, or do our best to escape our echoes, which are chambered like atria and ventricles in the heart.

That time I attend a strategy session at the Global Justice Center.

We're split into breakout groups and asked to sticky-note our political priorities on a whiteboard. People write down things like "reproductive health," "gay rights," "families at the border."

That time after workshop when Kelsey and I cook a San Pedro cactus in my kitchen. After several hours of peeling and de-spining the cactus, steaming it and then mashing it into a pulp, straining the green juice through a T-shirt, drinking said juice and eating said pulp, we go outside to a sandy wash by the interstate and wait.

That time nothing happens.

That time I spit into a vial so that a social scientist studying elections can assess voter stress levels. My compensation: fifty dollars and the regurgitation of a feeling.

That time I knock on Kelsey's door to catch a smoke and she is crying over another bitter familial dispute about politics. I stand with her, and cry too, and then we step outside for our smoke.

That time a boy I've been seeing takes me for a ride in his truck: the sky banded yellow and white, Yves Klein and quartz.

That time, at the women's march downtown, when I dream together with the crowd that an asymptote might arise, a line impossible for even the direst of political equations to cross, a line drawn by either human decency or just plain math—a line as imaginary as any transect, or border.

I keep on running my transect, even if I no longer trust its results. (M. Jacqui Alexander: "And since there is no crossing that is ever undertaken once and for all, this ontological imperative of making the world intelligible to ourselves is, of necessity, an enterprise that is ongoing.") I drive my line into another line, crossing the border at Nogales. The boy I've been seeing comes with me. Together, we experience the smoothness of our passage—a thirty-five-dollar charge for international car coverage, a brief, unmemorable exchange at the checkpoint. By evening, we are at the seaside, just west of Guaymas, eating fat oysters rimmed with brine. During the time of Chinese exclusion, a Chinese-Mexican man named José Chang operated a border-crossing scheme out of Guaymas. He taught desperate Chinese how to masquerade as Mexican laborers, who back then could move with relative freedom in and out of the US. He had them cut off their ponytails and dress in stereotypical mestizo garb, supplied them with fake Mexican papers, and taught them to say "*Yo soy Mexicano*" on repeat. Prior to Chang's racial counterfeiting system, many migrants rode the train lines from Guaymas to the border. Some played a most dangerous game, stowing away with transnational freight or in the iced-over vents of refrigerated cars. Others got off within a few dozen miles of the border and walked.

Something I've learned is that a transector has neither the time nor the power to levitate above his own line. Step by step, the study lengthens, observer bias impinging every result. One day, the researcher looks up from the desert floor to find he's actually inside of it, muddling the "objectivity" of his study. On that day, he can see at last that what separates him from this land is mere, but powerful, illusion. He resolves to make his own inferences, his own illusions. He will discover that ocotillo blooms work in a pinch if the drugs don't deliver, and that the river does flow on special occasions, and that all the beetles in the freezer come back to life in the end, hooked feet clawing at walls of ice.

My trip across the line is not very taxing. I sit for three days on the sun-burnished terrace of an empty hotel by the Gulf of California, trying to finish the essays in my thesis.

Maybe people will always believe in these imaginary lines. How fiercely they bristle with fences and checkpoints and drug-sniffing dogs is surely a testament to the steadfastness of such beliefs. I have to think it's possible, though, to imagine a line and not want to fix it in place. In the latter years of the nineteenth century, one of the surveyors who helped to draw up the official maps of the border, for reasons of ethics or greed, used his knowledge of the line to help Chinese migrants avert it. A person may walk a line in order to enforce it, to make it more solid and impermeable than before, but others will walk it for the opposite reason. They walk it and observe, secretly hoping they might one day breach this line and crack its equation, undoing the study and all its false assumptions.

Of course, not everything about a place can be known to he who walks a transect. How could one enumerate the serenities of daylight in the desert, the quiet fatalism of brush before the burn? C. D. Wright, in *Cooling Time*, writes, "What landscape is: not a closed space, not in fact capable of closure. With each survey the corners shift. Distance is the goal; groping, the means."

Right before we defend our theses, Kelsey and I decide to go out dancing. I put on very short shorts, a denim jacket, and a pair of leather sandals my ankles keep slipping out of. We each tongue a tab of acid and go from one club to the next, arms linked, our undercuts facing each other scalp to scalp. Out on Fourth Avenue, a man on a bender calls out, "Look, Chinese takeout!" I turn around to face him—and his friends, who are studiously ignoring our presence. The sidewalk looks bright to my dilated eyes, a stroke of orange I share with the man and his spiky hair, his clotted-cream complexion. The man puts his hand on my shoulder and asks me if I'm offended. Yes, I tell him, I am. He wants to know why. Did he get it wrong, am I not Chinese? Before I can answer, the man gets angry. He feels very inconvenienced by all this. He starts pushing his face closer and closer to mine, spittle spraying across my face, forcing me to cave backward against a wall. The man slurs at me, repeatedly, "What are you? What are you? What are you?"

My mouth is open, but men like this always answer their own questions: "You look like a queer fuck to me," he says, mumbling and then louder. He walks away, and then lunges back to try and grab me, prompting Kelsey and me to make a break for it. We cross the street, running, as the man stays on his side, yelling after us that the "queer fuck bar" is back the way we came.

What I miss most about Tucson is how dark the nights were. A local ordinance against light pollution ensured that the stars were always visible and that whatever artificial lights were allowed shone as brightly as beacons. Kelsey and I head for our crane. It has been many weeks since the election, but the crane is still electric, a bridge of light splitting the void. It is so beautiful, our crane. We do not think then of consequences or causes, of how that crane is there at the behest of a brand-name hotel chain, and that after we leave this city, the crane will go down and the hotel will go up, casting its shadow on the street, shuttering the café far below where we met to write down all our stories. But no, right now, we live in a sequence of unimpeachable moments. We live in that time when an asymptote arises, but still we cross the dance floor at the queer fuck club; that time on the rooftop when Solange plays for an hour-long minute; that time we look up and the crane is still there, still lit; that time by the tracks when the train cars that say *China Shipping Company* are passing, these boxes I want to climb back into; Tucson to LA, LA to Shanghai; the dream of a further crossing.

What are you? the man asks, but what I am is gone.

Love on the Rocks

I.

There is a tree on campus where all the lovers go. They deface this tree, carve their names into the wood and kill the tree slowly, for love. One day, I dreamed that we were there, and that you were as you always are—laid-back, sylvan, a little stingy with your words—while I stood beside you, hot with *shanghuo*—that inner heat my grandmother blames for my acne and my temper.

In the dream, we did not know what to do at the tree, like we lacked the proper tools or sentiment for each other to act. When I awoke, sticky and unresolved, it was already evening, and I was due to meet you at Casa Video, the rental palace and movie bar we go to every Friday to drink craft cider, and browse. There is an old-fashioned popcorn machine at Casa Video, as well as a nook upstairs stocked with foreign films. We checked out Zhang Yimou's *Hero*, and *In the Mood for Love* by Wong Kar-Wai. Both are love stories of a sort, though not particularly romantic ones. The first film ends with a couple's double suicide, the other in unconsummated desire. Funnily enough, the actors playing the foiled lovers are the same in both movies: Maggie Cheung opposite Tony Leung, their feelings for each other evergreen even as their prospects never get better.

In the movie whose treatment I've been writing in my head, a gay Asian man is riding the elevator up to your Tucson apartment, the one with the north-facing views of the train tracks and Mount Lemmon. He's been thinking lately about one of his first days in this city, how his key had refused to turn in the lock of a borrowed apartment. On that day, he'd sat down on the bristly welcome mat, watching an unknown neighbor do laps in the pool. Maybe love is always having that someone on the inside, ready to let you in, or maybe it's the doorframe that swells in the summer heat, catching a deadbolt fast. The man walked down to the pool and bought a cold Fanta from the vending machine. He put the can to the keyhole and waited for something to happen: a contraction in the frame, an answer to his open sesame.

2.

For years, I've kept a folder on my computer called "Love on the Rocks." Inside are photographs I take of lovers' marks: the carved or painted dedications to love one can find anywhere there are lovers. Most of the marks in my collection are small, containing nothing more than a phrase or a set of initials, two letters connected by a plus sign or an ampersand. Some lovers enclose their first names in entirety, though rarely their surnames. Many even date the mark, as if signing a contract.

Graphically speaking, most of these marks look messy or slipshod to me—what you'd expect from illicit jottings made in public. As one friend comments, the marks always look like the efforts of someone very young and stupid, someone in love.

3.

The basic message conveyed by each mark seems to be that *X and Y were in love at this place.* Because the story of their relationship can only appear here cursorily, we viewers are left to speculate. X might be saying they love Y unrequitedly, making the mark premature, even a little creepy, or maybe Y is commemorating a relationship already lost, in which case the mark says, *We were once together, but alas, no more.*

Whenever a mark catches my eye, I wonder where its author is now and if they're still making the same marks for the same person. I wonder, too: Why here on this wall, this barnacled piling beneath a pier? Was the mark's placement premeditated, or did it arise out of convenience? Each mark's style, or lack thereof, would certainly indicate a spur-of-the-moment decision, but who are all these people walking around with hammer and chisel, then, always primed to show their feelings with a cut?

Unlike all the texts, emails, and social media posts people use to discourse on love, each lovers' mark is left in a specific location, from a sidewalk in Minsk to a saguaro outside Tucson. The place a lover leaves their mark must say something about love's placement—its *situation*—in their life. Maybe they pick a place because it reminds them of a current or past lover in some potent, if inexplicable way, or maybe the tie is more direct: this is where they met, where they proposed, where they fooled around for the first time outside, behind the dumpster, his back against the brick.

Everyone seems to accept that love can just do this to us, making vandals out of romantics. Only a feeling as over-the-top as love could be so indecorous, and only love deserves, indeed demands, such exhibitionism. Part of me feels embarrassed for these mark makers, how demonstrative they insist on being with their feelings (feelings that will necessarily change, I snipe from the peanut gallery). But then there's that other part of me, the part that hangs on every text that you send, and that is considering, even now, what it'd be like to join that incorrigible crowd, to leave a synopsis of our love story (cringe) scribbled onto this Earth, out there for everyone to see.

4.

As linguistic acts devoted to love, the marks in my collection remind me of Roland Barthes's writing on the amorous "figure." Barthes's book *A Lover's Discourse: Fragments* is organized into eighty such figures, each a different way of performing, enacting, or otherwise expressing a feeling of love. In his preface, Barthes describes these figures as "gymnastic" feats; they are renditions of a lover's impassioned discourse, not attempts at defining love's essence. Barthes's book isn't a dictionary, it's a script, one tailored to the romantic "image-repertoire" of an erudite, and often lovesick, French theorist.

The lovers' marks in my collection are also, to quote Barthes, "outlined (like a sign) and memorable (like an image or a tale)." They are tactile texts, carved and not just typed. They exemplify Barthes's idea of love as a "scene of language," a scene in which words become material, a sensual object produced by the lovestruck body. "Language is a skin," Barthes writes. "I rub my language against the other."

5.

During my early twenties, I moved around a lot, sleeping with men and photographing marks. In Oslo, I found them jotted in Sharpie on the arched spine of a park bench right next to the Akerselva. In Osh, I found them branded, like permanent hickeys, into the rocks of a sacred mountain known as the Sulaiman-Too. In Nepal, the marks marshaled on a gazebo outside of Nagarkot, and in Hawaii, they scarred the banyan trees in Ala Moana Park. On Borneo, one rainy season, I hiked for hours on flooded trails to find a boulder marked by some long-departed couple. *L + E*, that sigil calculated, on an abacus slick with algae.

To me, the marks seemed like a useful metaphor for the kind of "love life" I was learning to lead. They, too, looked like isolated incidents, and yet, unlike my hookups, the marks had endured, outlasting their moment of inception by more than a few days. Although each of my encounters did make some impression on me, the men I met while traveling usually left nothing physical behind, no trace or reminder. I don't wish to belabor the point of modern "hookup culture." Among gay men of my generation, raised on Craigslist and Grindr, that culture sometimes feels like the only topic of our loving discourse, not to mention a focal point for self-flagellation and guilt. While traveling (and fucking), I honestly didn't think too much about it; I kept liking my first and final encounters with different men, the way I could bracket each one with a few telling details—S's whorl of auburn chest hair or D's junipery scent; the way my love life could, with each encounter, begin again.

6.

I remember walking once across a grassy knoll outside of Taipei. During World War II, the Japanese occupiers had built a series of pillbox fortifications on top of the hill, and as I stood before one of these structures, I could see a series of hearts and numbers scraped into its side like lines of romantic code, a cipher whose meaning I couldn't decrypt.

Later that night, I went to Aniki, a sprawling gay bathhouse located in a basement beneath the city. It was my first time patronizing such a business, so I remember it well: swiping through the turnstiles; shucking my clothes in the locker room; walking nude through a red-lit maze as hands grazed my thigh, my ass; refereeing a threesome with a PhD student from Canada and a taciturn DJ; feeling like I had too many places to be, too many cushioned cubicles with condom dispensers built into their walls, too many times when I thought I might leave, but then, another hand, another graze. Something kept drawing me back into the maze—my sex drive, surely, but something else as well. I felt possessed by the irrational belief that if I waited long enough, one of these strangers would stir in me more than just an anticipatory clenching of glutes. I would know him when I saw him. He would press up against me in the corridor, whispering words both sweet and confiding in my ear. He would leave on me a mark.

Early the next morning, still awake in that maze beneath the city, I met a doctor named Sky who lay with me beside a one-way mirror to watch the nude parade scroll past. Sky's distinguishing characteristic was the thermos of warm water he carried with him around the bathhouse—Barthes, in his notes from China, calls the water thermos a "fetish object" of the Chinese. After we cleaned ourselves off, Sky wrote his number on the back of a 7-Eleven receipt and told me to call him, though of course I never did.

7.

I won't pretend a switch flipped the night that we met—gay, monogamous love settling like a spotlight over us. Sitting outside the bar, we talked electoral politics and sipped our vodka sodas. I remember noting the slim fall of your shadow, the nautical tattoos half-covered by your sleeve. "He isn't really my type," I would say to my friends later, a dodge as much as a dismissal.

8.

Hard as we may try to turn our love lives into a private territory, a lease shared by just a *you* and a *me*, love is also a commons, a busy street we split with a *them*. Like most Americans, I grew up in a commons dominated by representations of straight-white-people love, a love that looked nice and expensive from the outside, but also quite vapid. I resented the omnipresence of *that* love, the love of homecoming courts and *Sex and the City*, parking lot hanky-panky and *Dawson's Creek*, and yet I also couldn't deny how attractive I found its panoply of images. If you didn't know this about me already, you will soon enough: I have always been an avid consumer of Hollywood rom-coms and Top Forty ballads. I have watched *Under the Tuscan Sun* an alarming number of times (in my non-director's cut, it's Sandra Oh, the pregnant Asian sidekick, and not Diane Lane who leaves for Italy on a midlife romantic hajj). I'm not well versed in the Beatles or Beach Boys or anything remotely classic, but I can sing, off-tune, every bar of every Goo Goo Dolls song, and sometimes when I'm sad, I'll play Train's 2001 megahit "Drops of Jupiter" on my phone as I do the dishes and dance about my kitchen. Such fluff composes probably ninety-nine percent of my loving discourse, my script. If I ever muster the courage to say, "I love you," I'll be saying it partly through them.

9.

The lovers' marks I've collected aren't afraid to be cheesy or trite. Perhaps this is one lesson I could take from them—the need to shrug off my elitism, to try phrasing my love in the simplest possible terms. *I need you. I want you. My baby. My love.*

In the weeks following our first meeting, I'd drag my friends to the dance floor every time a Taylor Swift song played. Taking a piss at a café, I'd smile stupidly at the bathroom walls lavished in hearts and names. And at the movie theater, love's library and its church, I'd watch every square-jawed actor emote to his shiny-haired love interest, and then I would bike downtown to your apartment as fast as I could, thinking I was the shiny-haired love interest tonight.

10.

It seems telling that most of my early experiences with sex and love happened while I was living out of a suitcase. The men I "connected with" on Grindr didn't beat around the bush. After a flurry of pictorial exchanges to verify mutual interest, they would ask if I wanted to "host" or "travel." My answer was always the latter.

Over the years, I've sometimes felt like a seedy sex tourist compiling an international rolodex of quick fucks. I worry that I am treating each lover too much like a prop and not the complicated, amorous figure they surely must be. In more charitable moods, I try and think of each hookup as just another ambiguous window on whatever place I am visiting. I learned from a police officer in Jinghong, for instance, about the platonic love he felt for his best friend, a lesbian graphic designer he planned on marrying as his beard, and I learned from a restaurateur in Mostar about all the queer Bosnians who regularly took jobs on international cruise liners to make money and get laid. In Copenhagen, a Russian photographer I met at a bar taught me which of my facial angles best caught the light (afterward, he also fucked my face). In chilly, early-summer Oslo, I drank tea and listened to an exchange student from Dar es Salaam wax nostalgic about beaches and tan lines and the men with deep brown eyes waiting beneath the fronds.

I wouldn't be surprised to learn that many of my lovers' tales were as fabricated or embellished as my own. Depending on the trip, I could be a Chinese native working in Beijing, a newly minted expat, a naive biology student, a wannabe writer on vacation—all accurate biographies to some extent. It can be alarmingly easy to slip in and out of a life when spending time with people you don't expect to meet again, easy to discard, if only temporarily, your accountability to the facts.

I would like to think that the act of loving these men, or at least loving the places these men took me, has helped propel me through the world, from mark to mark and tryst to tryst. If this is true, then the motion must go, must cut, both ways. Just as I have tried to take brief excursions through my encounters, I have been, for some of these men at least, a short stay in an exotic land, a veranda bathed in oriental sun. These men have toured me, and I have transited them in turn, each of us seeking some congress with difference, each of us tireless in our search.

II.

What about you, then? The you who is unfailingly polite and secularly Jewish and almost exactly my height. The you who grew up in

Arizona and stayed there for college. The you who sat by rectangles of turquoise water each summer in high school, a lifeguard employed by the city of Phoenix. The you with your cactus stud earring and your beat-up Tacoma.

I am trying to fit brackets on you as I have all the others, to render you a charming bit of terroir. But when we met, I was also residing inside these same brackets—your place in the world was more to me, that is, than just a pit stop. I couldn't easily skirt it, nor you. Once, while on a date with another guy I was seeing, I ran into you on the street. You called out to me, and we joined you, and after a round of very casual-seeming introductions, I had to spend the next hour hanging out with you and the other guy, telling myself this was definitely normal, because it wasn't like either of you wanted to be my boyfriend, or anything cheesy like that.

In retrospect, I realize it may seem like I was playing hard to get, even though, in my mind, I was following the protocols of post-monogamy gay life. No man my age who dated men was supposed to ask for commitment; no one seemed to want or need such bounds. And yet I was waking up every other morning in your bed and pouring myself coffee from your French press, just as I was meeting you each Friday at Casa Video so we could raid the celluloid stacks. I never found the idea of being your boyfriend unpalatable—far from it—but the idea of a real relationship seemed far-fetched. My plan had always been to move back to China after my graduate program ended, a plan I shared with you on our first date. Because of this, it seemed almost irresponsible to spend our weekends cuddled up on your couch, watching movies. We watched *Millennium Mambo* and *Three Times* by Hou Hsiao-hsien, *Summer Palace* by Lou Ye, Tsai Ming-liang's *The River*, and every movie ever made by Jia Zhangke and Wong Kar-Wai.

Screening these films was a crash course for both of us in contemporary Asian cinema, but also, perhaps, a sidelong way of showing you where I was going and inviting you to come with me.

12.

The truth is I've always felt like a novitiate when it comes to matters of the heart—a Phaedrus, I'm always looking for my Socrates. My uncertainty stems in part from how difficult it has been for Asian men in America, whether straight, gay, or neither, to see themselves as romantic protagonists. This is not to say we all feel unlovable, sexually deprived, ugly, or repugnant (though a contingent of us very vocally do); it's to say that when we are loved or desired, when someone fucks us and wants to keep doing it repeatedly, like a tic, when we're held up as a paragon of anything other than braininess and hard work, when we play, onstage or in life, people hemorrhaging emotions and not just Zen koans, people who are open holes rather than obdurate sphincters, who have enterprising genitalia instead of Ken Watanabe–esque blanks, and who definitely aren't here to dispense wisdom, or consult on web design, or lodge racially cucked, misogynist, "Isn't it crazy how Asian girls only date white guys?" jokes from the sidelines—when any of this happens, it seems like a mistake, and inside our cold, cold hearts in our insensate fleshbot bodies, we suddenly don't know how to feel anymore.

If being romantically or sexually desired is not a cultural given, then love becomes an attainment, even a status symbol: to be the loved one amidst the unloved.

13.

Here I am, then, a body marked, and waiting, for love: rail-thin and hairless except for the dark thatches under my arms; tan, acne-prone skin with a smattering of tattoos; long legs and exceedingly bony arms.

In America, but also abroad, this package tends to attract middle-aged white men with watery Anglo features who refer to themselves, not unproudly, as "rice queens." I've definitely gone home with such men before, the international business types who carry pictures of blond nephews and nieces in their wallets. More often than not, on dance floors and dating apps, I am drawing these men's attention; I am a connoisseur, you might say, of their type.

The handful of Asian men I've slept with while traveling often ask me about American men, by which they mean white men like you. To them, I am a foreign correspondent, a member of their team with privileged access to the average American male. My Asian lovers want to know about cock size and eye color and hair that erroneously curls. They ask me what it's like to be fucked by a man like that, taking for granted, as I do, that my preferences swing that way. I find it difficult to tell whether these men are envious of me, or if they find my accounts of interracial intimacy depressing. Within gay porn and the few other cultural venues in which gay Asian American men are portrayed, "Asian and anus are conflated," observes the artist Richard Fung. The gay Asian American male, when deemed erotic at all, is desired for his lithe recumbency, his impressive ability to receive, especially when the received article is not Asian.

14.

I am not here to rail against the credo of "personal preference," or to forward some radical campaign for a society-wide redistribution of love that would conveniently work in my favor. I am just another confused resident of an amorous commons whose dominant "image-repertoire" has been constructed without bodies and backgrounds like my own in mind, or else with a stereotype standing in as my double. Being a social animal like anyone else, I cannot help but want to get with this program, to love with the same easy rectitude I see projected all around me on television screens and advertisements. More often than I am comfortable discussing, getting with this program has meant getting with whiteness, and making him love me as much as I can.

When I first met you, I was surprised to learn that none of your previous boyfriends had been Asian; your interest in me, that is, did not follow a predilection. I know that love in its unalloyed form—true love, that good shit, the shit honored by every lovers' mark I photograph—is supposed to supersede all such quibbles about age, race, and other demographic factors. One of love's promissory conditions, after all, is that it shall take the generalized like one feels for certain people (in my case gay, usually white, cis-men) and hone that feeling down to something individuated, a bell that tolls only for the infinitesimal particulars of the one I love, the singular, implausible, *you*. And yet the anxieties I feel about my qualifications and deficits as a lover, or loved object, remain. I cannot help but still see us as others might, as one of those Asian male–white guy pairings ubiquitous today on the streets of Cambridge or Brooklyn. How can I critique exoticism when my own, colored body seems exotic to me? When I trade on its currency of difference and am, in general, pleased with the returns?

15.

Perhaps a better, or at least answerable, question to ask is "Are we sluts?" Carrie Bradshaw famously asks this on an episode of *Sex and the City* after many stymied attempts at getting into new beau Aidan's pants. She wonders what the modern woman has given up in exchange for no longer waiting before sex. "Romance!" Carrie crows to Miranda as they stroll around Central Park. "I'm telling you it didn't even occur to me, which is so depressing!"

Did I forget about romance when I took you home after a few too many drinks that first night? Or when I gave head to a bi-curious German in an Auckland bathroom? Or when a grad student in Somerville told me I looked like his Burmese twink dream, but I slept with him anyway, spread-eagled on his waist?

I find it difficult to consider this question in the way that Carrie et al intended it—as an inquiry into my moral condition, my prudery or my sin. Without glamorizing promiscuity too much, I want to say that by loving in this way, I have tried and sometimes even succeeded at falling for the men who come and then go, these men who take you to sheer cliffs of feeling and leave you there, all breathy and out of sorts. I have been one of these men to other men, I hope. I have pulled them into rapid closeness and then let them back out into the night, and in the morning, if they're still around, I've wondered, as we all do, bashfully, to ourselves: *What would it look like if he stayed?*

16.

At the end of each encounter, there is always a moment of retraction, of staring down what Barthes calls the "long tunnel" that follows each love affair's instigating moment. My limbs untangle from his. I wash up in the bathroom, get dressed, smile because I've seen this "scene of language" before.

I don't think sleeping around is the only or even the best way to figure out what love is or can be. My encounters have, if anything, taught me more about what love isn't than what it is, each hookup a teaser trailer for some unfeasible future. It wasn't love (but an exercise in self-sabotage) when I got on the back of a partnered man's bike in Shanghai one summer. It wasn't love (but a resurgent kleptomania) when I left another man's apartment in Milan with a photograph swiped from his bookshelf. It wasn't love (but a reckless kind of loneliness) when I let a man twice my age pick me up beside a Montanan lake, get me high, and fix me a Boston Market TV dinner in his trailer camper. It certainly wasn't love when this man came, shuddering over my pliant, vacated shape, how the pot and booze made me feel like I was slipping away through the air, my borders fuzzy and indistinct. Later, I would grope my way as if blindfolded through the dark insides of this man's life. I would find the door, the fence in the grass, the road outside leading somewhere new.

17.

It wasn't love the night we met, but it didn't preclude the option, either. Like two obliging weather systems, we developed in line with the forecast: hipster bar, cheap drinks, the quiet walk at midnight back to my place.

After you left, I sat on my stoop, trying to remember exactly the way you had descended my body, how I had ascended yours in response. We had exited the scene but left the door open. You would come back often, standing at my cusp, asking in your own words to enter.

18.

Part of my trouble with love is how stubbornly I cling to my own subjectivity, to the knowledge that these vignettes, these marks, are mine alone to inhabit and record. The stranger who is my lover retains the status of a character in each encounter. I can sympathize with him, care for him, maybe even love him, but he need never follow me out the door, back into the clutches of all that is quotidian and daily.

On the other hand, the time I've spent with you is nothing if not a series of moments interpretable from both sides. I remember an early date when you came over so we could watch Wong Kar-Wai's queer classic *Happy Together* from 1997. Lying on the carpet of my unfurnished apartment, we watched the film's central lovers—two gay Chinese men caught in a codependent, toxic relationship—dance the tango in their dilapidated Argentine kitchen. That image is the film's crucial amorous figure: Leslie Cheung finally closing his eyes, sated, as Tony Leung holds him close. You were so quiet through that almost brutally romantic moment that I wished to compare notes, to be consenting adults in the way one of my college professors used to talk about consent. One day, after another long exegesis on Plato, she looked up from her slides and told the class, sotto voce, that *consent* comes from the Latin *consentir*, or together-feel, and so to consent to a person is to agree to feel together with them, to be as porous to that person and their feelings as one person can be. I remember thinking this was the most romantic etymology I'd ever heard, and I also remember, years later, looking at you in my apartment and asking you what you thought of that scene.

19.

Consenting to love does not mean melding with your partner into gloopy oneness—love is neither telepathy nor fondue. But still, in love, the other person can't be avoided, exited like a place, or negotiated into obeisance. A powerful decentering has begun to occur, so that even my language, my discourse, preserves pieces of you. I have become all too aware of your location, how proximate or distant it is from mine. I have begun, grudgingly, to participate in what Alain Badiou thinks love should be: two individuals trying to reconcile (but not necessarily solve) their disjoint experiences of the world. "You have Two," Badiou writes. "Love involves Two."

20.

Returning to the photos in my folio, I notice that the lovers' marks recur in places where two entities meet in some kind of discord or harmony. Romantic vandals leave their marks at the Grand Canyon, where red earth cleaves into blue sky, and at Niagara Falls, where Canada abuts America. The lovers go to Stanley Market, in Hong Kong, to sprinkle their names on the tide line, and they haunt the grounds at Dunkirk and Manassas, where opposed forces once met in mutually assured destruction.

I don't know yet whether our doubleness needs such memorial, if I should be taking my penknife and paints to the backlot of that rental palace off Speedway where every Friday we used to meet. For so long, I have thought about love as a feeling that lives and dies in the moment. I have thought about love through the words of philosophers like Barthes and Badiou rather than poets like Audre Lorde—Lorde, who writes, breathlessly describing a lover's touch, "I am come home."

What I have avoided thinking about too deeply is the hope I hold in sync with Lorde's words, the hope that we will not disappear into or away from each other, that we will keep our separateness but stay somehow a unit, moving through the world in each other's company, each other's co-feeling. I do not balk at the cliché this figure enacts: love as two people's shared journey, a long march through city and fen. It makes me think of a time a few years ago, in Manchuria, when I watched a group of lovers cast red paper lanterns over a frozen river. There was a bridge in that city covered in thousands of lovers' marks. I spent hours picking over the bridge as carefully as I could, wanting to record each and every one. Standing at the bridge's center that night, I looked over the railing and saw a flock of lanterns detach from the river's southern bank. The lanterns floated on unsure winds to the river's other side, where they fell into the snowdrifts as trash.

Chinese love is so often typecast as the honoring of a pledge or the fulfillment of a child's filial duties. The lanterns over that Chinese river said love differently, though. That love's figure was uncontrolled, the result of an inexpert heave made in the night. That love traveled, shaking on queer winds: flickering, but holding.

21.

One of Barthes's most wildly romantic claims is that love cannot be measured in terms of safety or risk. "But how can you *evaluate* viability? Why is the viable a Good Thing? Why is it better to *last* than to *burn*?" These questions, they wail.

There are days when I want to burn it all down, this flimsy construction we have made of ourselves, but there are other days when

I want to lounge forever with you in these rooms, petting the shiny skin of your words, dreaming of a tree we might still etch. More and more, I find it difficult to believe in any of the binaries I have tried to see in the marks—these dyads of singleness and doubleness, adventure and fidelity, all we imagine and all that has been imagined for us. By trying to discipline love into clear and legible categories, I've mostly just discovered the obvious: that both marginal marks and French philosophers make for poor romantic teachers, however elegant their formulations.

22.

We are flickering still, we are holding. It was you who finally asked me to make it official. We were standing on a rooftop, splitting a cigarette and a beer. You told me you knew that the timing wasn't great, what with my move fast approaching, but many relationships start out premised on planned obsolescence, and some of those relationships don't stick to their plan. Maybe you could visit me in China, and we could take it from there; I said yes, I would like that. A few weeks later, after you'd left for a summer job counting goshawks in Utah, I packed up my Tucson apartment and drove home to Tennessee, a one-way ticket to China already booked in my name.

At the end of *Happy Together*, the two men are no longer in love. Or maybe they are in love, but their co-feeling is no longer supportable. Tony goes home to Hong Kong, leaving Leslie behind in Buenos Aires, curlicues of cigarette smoke adorning his lips.

"Why are the movies you show me always so sad?" you once asked me. I don't know, but I haven't ruled out our happier ending just yet.

23.

Ultimately, the marks I collect are made by lovers for their lovers, not for me, this voyeur come from the future. Whatever is transmitted by each mark is publicly available but privately held, a message meant for one person, alone.

It was I who first said the words to you, during that long summer when I was no longer living in Tucson but hadn't yet moved to the East. I drove across the country to say them, because it seemed like the most romantic possible way. As the states between us passed—Missouri, Nebraska, Wyoming, Utah—I vacillated about how exactly to say it. All I could think about was that moment in many Wong Kar-Wai films when a person in love will whisper something into a mud-filled hole in a wall, a knot in a tree, or a friend's tape recorder. What words the lovers speak in these scenes are never divulged, and indeed do not matter. The point is that the lovers are speaking, and that we are seeing, but not fully comprehending, the act of expression as it takes shape.

24.

Once, after many days alone with myself, I came to a town near what geographers call the "Eurasian Pole of Inaccessibility," otherwise known as the most inland point on Earth. There were no tourists in this town, just goatherds and truck drivers and people like me who came for the pleasure of passing through. I didn't know where exactly in the desert the Pole was located, but like any hopeless romantic, I longed to get as close to the inaccessible as I could. After an hour or so of walking, I came to a rocky tor jutting up from the desert and decided to climb it before turning around. I expected to stand at the top, contemplating my solitude while looking out over the vast and tawny desert. Instead, I saw smokestacks and train cars and the ragged edges of the town I had just left. I could also see, between tor and town, a giant, bilingual lovers' mark that some couple had left there in all of life's heat and isolation: a sign meant for you, and for me, but mostly for them.

Letter from Manhattan 2

Is there sense in the sentiment? Is being a citizen of the world—a "cosmopolitan," in the word's root sense—something one can, or should, aspire to?

—KWAME ANTHONY APPIAH

Two things happened to me right before I moved to China for the second time: I fell in love, and I witnessed a solar eclipse. The first experience caught me by surprise and basically unhinged me, so that for the three months I spent apart from L that summer, I could not be counted on to write sentences, or buy groceries, or maintain casual conversations with friends. All I could do was think about L, and pine, a state of abject need I and everyone around me found, in a word, intolerable.

The second experience required protective eyewear and was planned to a T. I knew exactly when during the day on August 21, 2017, the moon was scheduled to intercede between our planet and its star, and where I should be when that happened. Both events were, in their own way, total—I was not the same person afterward. In both cases, I was utterly unprepared, gobsmacked, a clammy-skinned ball of emotions reeling about in the kind of directionless dusk that only an infrequent celestial event or something approximate, like falling in love for the first time, can conjure. Bands of shadow quivered like muscles on the lake water. I looked up at the sky, sobbing at the stupid, inarticulate fullness in me. I gave in to it, and then it ended, and I was a cogent and mobile person once more.

Experiencing these two events in short order made moving to China again feel almost mundane in comparison. Growing up, I'd visited relatives in the country on a regular basis and had spent the better part of a year there right after college. L, on the other hand, had never set foot outside of the United States, save for three nights in Mexico we both decided not to count. At that point in our relationship, he and I had only been dating a few months. That I'd asked him to uproot his life to a foreign country for me felt like a titanic imposition; that he'd actually agreed was a miracle, or else the trump card of all romantic gestures, one as stupid as it was brave.

By the end of that summer, we were living in Chengdu, a city of fourteen million known for its spicy food and proximity to pandas. Chengdu has been a cultural and economic linchpin of China's interior since at least 310 BC, when records first indicate the emergence of something resembling a city at the heart of the Chengdu Plain. As with pretty much all of China's cities, very few physical reminders of Chengdu's antiquity remain. In the 1600s, a regional warlord named Zhang Xianzhong overthrew the ruling Ming dynasty and wrested control of what is today Sichuan Province for himself, only to lose it later to the advancing Manchus. Xianzhong burnt Chengdu and most of its inhabitants to the ground in retreat, and so the Qing rebuilt the city as a walled imperial outpost surrounded by rivers on three sides, with a soldiers' garrison near the west gate, brothels near the east, municipal buildings at its center, and silk filatures producing the region's famed brocades scattered about the perimeter. Repopulated by migrants from across Sichuan and southern China, Chengdu gained a reputation for welcoming outsiders and encouraging indulgence—a reputation it retains to the present day. Chengduers supposedly loathe working and love to entertain. It is the kind of place a young person goes to disappear, or to put their plans on ice for a while.

When my grandparents moved to Chengdu in the early seventies, the Qing-era city had also disappeared without a trace, leveled by redevelopment in addition to Japanese bombs. My apo and agong have lived for as long as I can remember in a tenement building just off Yi Huang Lu (First Ring Road), not far from where the city walls used to loom. Their building has the shape, coloring, and overall charisma of a cinder block. Almost all the families who live in their complex originally came from Shanghai, and all the heads of household used to work in the same factory. The apartments themselves are also nearly identical: two rooms, one for living and the other for sleeping, plus a cramped annex in between that includes a kitchen and a small washroom. My mother came of age in this city, and Chengdu is where her parents have chosen to stay. When I was born, my mother picked the second half of my Chinese name, Nuocheng, to honor that association.

For me, Chengdu represented more of an exit, or a convenient deferral, than a homecoming. National politics in the country of my birth had been skewing rightward since Trump's election, especially when it came to outsiders, immigrants, or anything to do with "CHAI-nuh," a word our new president used like an epithet. I was well aware that Xi Jinping's China was no better, no lower down on the scale of chauvinistic ethnonationalisms, but as I joked to L at the time, at least the politburo was more consistent and purposeful in its authoritarianism—here in China, there was not even the imprint of a functioning national democracy to feel disillusioned by. In any case, I wasn't trying to defect from one maddening nation to another; I was trying to build a life somehow external to that binary choice, a life that refused to choose a side because there were no defensible sides to choose.

Perhaps it is only fitting, then, that L and I would spend the bulk of our time in Chengdu lounging about an apartment complex known as Manhattan 2, surfing the web using a VPN service that made it seem like we were in Brisbane—that is, neither here nor there. I loved our Manhattan-but-not apartment. I loved the shell-like tub inside the bathroom's minimalist glass cube, the shiny red cabinetry, the two stories connected by a floating staircase, the garden where I hung up our his-and-his laundry, the floor-to-ceiling windows on both sides that made the most of Chengdu's anemic light, the absurd fact that we paid two hundred dollars a month for all this. Our apartment had been Tetris-ed into a high-rise shaped like an openwork concrete grid, with multiple units stacked in each massive quadrangle. The building reminded me of Louis Sachar's Wayside School, in that the elevator only stopped on every third floor, and the rain fell on some terraces and not others. There was even a wing of the building that looked deserted, overgrown with ferns and frangipani. A skybridge connected us to that mystery quarter, but the bridge had no accessible entry point, and the first time I went looking for one, I wound up on the roof, surrounded by belching pipes and soft pats of moss.

For one entire year, L and I did not cook our own meals or regularly check our social media accounts, which were blocked, or think in any constructive way about our "careers." We worked sporadic hours at English training schools for bosses who didn't care if we had the right visas or not, periodically leaving and then reentering the country to reset the clock on our stays. When we returned from these jaunts, we always went down to the Public Security Bureau to reregister as resident aliens with the sharply dressed ladies who worked there, the ladies who referred to us as their "favorite men of leisure."

In *xiuxian*, leisurely Chengdu, L and I were always dozing off in the back of some cab, late at night, as we headed home from another round of hot pot and drinks. Every cab in the city would play the same greeting to signal your trip had begun: "Welcome to Chengdu, a new global city, home of the panda!" As that city yawed into motion outside, I'd watch little galaxies of neon light collect and then fade on L's face. My hand would find his on the seat, hazarding a squeeze. "Where are you going again?" the driver would inquire, uncoupling our hands. I'd tell him to take us to Manhadun Er on Xinxiwan Lu, because that was where we lived that year: ten stories above a road named for "New Hope."

> Why should we think of people from China as our fellows the minute they dwell in a certain place, namely the United States, but not when they dwell in a certain other place, namely China?
>
> —MARTHA NUSSBAUM

WHAT WAS I DOING IN CHENGDU? PUT SIMPLY, I WAS TRYING TO align myself with the world rather than one of its many nations. This hope has many names, but philosophers like to call it "cosmopolitanism." Within the Western tradition, cosmopolitanism is usually traced to Diogenes of Sinope, who, when asked to identify his origins, supposedly said that he was "*kosmoupolites*," or "a citizen of the world." Cosmopolitans like to subscribe to the greatest and most all-encompassing of identity categories, our planet. For them, people are Earthlings first; everything else—whether we be Berbers or Jains, anti-vaxxers or ornithologists, bisexual Berliners or Singhalese-speaking, non-denominational Christian residents of Dubai—comes second.

The writer Kwame Anthony Appiah, one of cosmopolitanism's most eloquent modern proponents, subdivides the philosophy into "moral" and "cultural" strains. Moral cosmopolitanism is basically Liberalism 101—it concerns itself with the inalienable rights accorded to every person and the basic allotments of respect and care we owe one another regardless of creed, race, sex, et cetera. Meanwhile, cultural cosmopolitanism extols the glorious mixology of global art forms and social movements—the influence, for example, of Japanese ukiyo-e prints on European Impressionism in the nineteenth century, or the late-twentieth-century transmission of American hip-hop music and street style (themselves the progeny of prior cultural admixing) to the banlieues of Paris or the discotheques of Lagos. Both strains must exist for any cosmopolitan ethos to hold sway. They are the all-important addends of an equation that Appiah sums up as "universality plus difference." To uphold cosmopolitanism is to underscore the similitude of the human condition. At the same time, cosmopolitans generally seem to prefer open societies steeped in hybridity, as if it were only from such amalgams that any meaningful unity can be extracted.

Thinking about the world through a cosmopolitan lens enjoyed something of a renaissance in the nineties, a decade in which simultaneously ecstatic and anxious visions of a globalized world order flourished inside the academy. People learned from reading Francis Fukuyama that history had closed up shop at the end of the Cold War, and they learned from reading David Harvey that the world was getting perceptually smaller and more compressed. For those of us born into that time between the two falls—that of the Berlin Wall in 1989 and the Twin Towers in 2001—cosmopolitanism has often been easy to mistake for globalization. To try my hand at disambiguation, globalization is the modern process by which economies and political systems become more global in scale and interconnected in practice. Cosmopolitanism is instead an ancient theory for how to viably live as a world citizen. The latter is a hypothetical pursuit that the former has turned into a practical concern. Many boosters of globalization assumed that a more globalized world would naturally result in a more cosmopolitan one as well, a world where social and cultural differences were respected even as our commonalities rose to the fore. After a long twentieth century riven by ethnic and national conflicts, this seemed like an undisputable win: a geography of separate spheres and quarrelsome nations replaced by one of international collaboration, open borders, and acronymous organizations like NAFTA and the IMF.

A few months before I moved to China, the Harvard professor and former adviser-to-presidents Graham Allison published a book on US–China relations arguing against such rose-tinted narratives. Globalization had not healed geopolitical fault lines, paving the way to cosmopolitan peace. If anything, globalization had set the stage for a new era of international conflict by enabling China's rise from impoverished vassal state to world's second-largest economy, thus threatening America's prized role as Earth's military and economic hegemon. In *Destined for War: Can America and China Escape Thucydides's Trap?* Allison analogizes the current tensions between China and America to a time in the fourth century BC, when an ascendant Athens challenged Greece's reigning power, Sparta, for regional dominance, sparking thirty years of intensive fighting. China is the Athens of today, by Allison's reckoning, and America its Sparta.

The two countries' jockeying for power, and the war that may ensue, fits a paradigm that Allison has named "Thucydides's Trap" after the historian who wrote the *History of the Peloponnesian War*. (Like the cosmopolitans, Allison turns to the ancient Greeks to give credence to his pronouncements on the present, though in his case, what's being legitimized is an inclination toward conflict rather than a notion of world citizenship.) Allison doesn't think that war between China and America is "inevitable," even if most of the examples he cherry-picks from history seem to imply that it is. Per Allison's thesis, one nation of people cannot rise up in the world without another nation viewing them as an existential threat, and any war that results is not so much a failure of diplomacy or a steroidal derangement of human nature as it is the rational outcome of separate nations seeking a competitive edge.

Allison reproduces in his book a two-column graph outlining America and China's "clash of civilizations." According to this graph, America lives in the presentist "Now," whereas China's history encompasses all of "Eternity." America thinks of government as a "Necessary evil," while China views its overlords as a "Necessary good." The American state conducts itself as a "Missionary" would, seeking to impose its values upon all; in contrast, China sees itself as "Inimitable," without peer. For most of my life, I have carried around a similar graph in my mind. On the American side, I have placed language, sexual openness, art and self-expression, racism but also civil liberty. To China I have ceded family and blood, food and gathering, racial belonging cut by cultural opacity, social conformity, and silence. At some point, I started wanting to know what traits straddled this graph, or maybe more accurately, why I couldn't draw an expansive circle around all of it (all of me) and leave the fastidious parsing to Allison and other interested parties.

Maybe that's just my own delusion, though, the same delusion I've been laboring under since at least 2010, when I came to China for the first time as an adult to attend the World's Fair in Shanghai. I remember feeling overwhelmed by the scene and the crowds that day: all the pavilions shaped like beached whales and quivering pincushions; all the Chinese people lining up outside "Italy" and "Mexico" and "France." But I was also excited, honored even, to be a Chinese American alone and unhyphenated at last in this newly cosmopolitan country. It was a moment of external dilation that somehow helped me feel more connected to the world, like here I was, at the busiest World's Fair in recent memory, situated in one place that was also a microcosm for all the other places. I could see myself then as a partly finished product of that world, a world of burgeoning openness and hopelessly crossed wires. My lights were finally on, cosmopolitanism condensing into architecture all around me. I would keep coming back—to China, to the fair. I would keep chasing that worldly feeling.

> Perhaps real cosmopolitans, after they have taken out membership in that category, are never quite at home again, in the way real locals can be.
>
> —ULF HANNERZ

PRETTY MUCH EVERYONE L AND I KNEW IN CHENGDU HAD ALSO come to the city from somewhere else. At the English training schools where we worked, our colleagues had passports from Poland and Lithuania, South Africa and Belarus. My boss had grown up in New Mexico, though he'd spent the better part of the last decade in China, long enough to father two sons and start a teaching business with a

Chinese woman he was in the process of divorcing. In Manhattan 2, L and I lived right above a trio of sandy-haired Californians, or maybe Canadians who'd lived for a time in Oakland (I couldn't keep their story straight). The "Cocktail Boys," as we called them, kept longhorn cattle skulls and two unused surfboards on their terrace. They were distractingly handsome in the right lighting, which made their entrepreneurial enterprise, a custom cocktail delivery service called Nova, seem less asinine than it was.

And then there was Kristen, a kiwi of Chinese descent I'd met three years earlier while hitchhiking down the Karakoram Highway. Back then, Kristen had been studying Mandarin at Sichuan University; now she was a Chengdu local, not quite *bendiren* but definitely more embedded than your usual expat. Kristen worked as an event promoter for an arts venue downtown. She produced music and deejayed, mixing her own electronic tracks that sampled nineties R&B alongside Uyghur hip-hop. Known on stage as Kaishandao, Kristen was a fixture on Chengdu's underground music scene, a gadfly who rapped a strong flow with every bouncer, barback, and strung-out club kid in her large but chummy circle. While living in Chengdu, I would sometimes read Kristen's blog, *Kiwese*, where she posted album reviews, tour dates, and the occasional pensive reflection on life in Chengdu. I found her writing on cross-cultural issues refreshingly frank, even—or especially—when the content wasn't cheery. It was heartening to know that even one of those people who seemed to move so effortlessly through the world also felt the friction of her transit. "It tests me to be confident in myself," she wrote once, "to remember where I've come from (an isolated set of islands in the Pacific Ocean) and where my ancestors have come from (rural villages in southern China), and to have patience."

I, too, was trying to have patience—with myself, and with Chengdu. I aspired to feel comfortable here, to find my own routine within cosmopolitanism. At least once a month, L and I would have lunch with my grandmother at a KFC by her apartment. We'd eat spicy drumsticks shellacked in grease as Apo looked on, an expression of contented disgust on her face (a longtime Buddhist vegan, my apo nonetheless insisted on taking us to eat "American food" whenever we visited her). After each meal, we'd walk about the neighborhood, noting the new construction—the city was building its seventh subway line right in front of her building—as Apo kept telling me different versions of the same advice: it was nice I'd come here to Chengdu, but I should hasten back to my studies in America when I was done with my "break."

Apo didn't really understand what I was doing in China, or who this *laowai* was who kept crashing our lunches. I called L my "roommate" or "friend" when introducing him to Chinese relatives. Being explicit about our relationship seemed like too much trouble—not for me, but for my mother, who'd field most of the questions and bear most of the blame. In any case, I didn't see my relatives enough to make it into an issue. We lived in separate worlds within the same city. At the end of each visit, I'd walk my grandmother up the five flights of stairs to her apartment and say a quick hello-goodbye to my agong as L waited down on the street. (Apo didn't like anyone outside the family seeing how squalid their apartment had become.) Now that my agong was bedridden, hooked up to an oxygen concentrator to help with his worsening COPD, these two rooms measured the entire diameter of his life as well as hers.

"Do you think it's terrible I don't visit them more?" I asked L once, as we rode in the cab back to Manhattan 2. Now that I lived just twenty minutes away from my grandparents, staying away was a matter of choice as opposed to distance. "You're not a terrible person," he told me. "You've just got a lot on your plate."

> Difficult as it may seem to make a plural for "cosmos," it is now assumed more and more that worlds, like nations, come in different sizes and styles. Like nations. Worlds too are "imagined."
>
> —PHENG CHEAH AND BRUCE ROBBINS

WHEN PUT INTO PRACTICE, THE COSMOPOLITANISM ESPOUSED by critics like Appiah and exemplified by people like Kristen is all about making "conversation—and, in particular, conversation between people from different ways of life." In Chengdu, I was compensated by the hour to sit in a rambling apartment in Tongzilin my boss had turned into our "school," simulating these conversations for the children of well-off elites. Most of my students were studying for their TOEFL exams so that they could attend high school or college in the US. During our private lessons, I'd ask them questions about their hobbies and their family life, and then I'd help them translate their answers into what seemed like a suitably Western response.

Oscar was my favorite student—Oscar, who liked wearing Off-White sneakers and vacationing in Siem Reap and who rolled his eyes whenever I gave him printouts of *New York Times* articles about the clearing of migrant worker settlements outside of Beijing. Oscar's father was high up in the provincial government. His mother ran a local hospital. The goals he set for himself were the same ones set by all my students: entry into a tony New England prep school, followed preferably by Harvard. But unlike the others, Oscar also had a casualness to him, or perhaps just a better grasp of conversational English. He liked to sit around after class and gab with his teachers about soccer and internet ephemera, so much so that I started worrying he wasn't socializing enough with kids his own age—like many Chinese students looking to study abroad, Oscar had stopped attending his regular Chinese school, putting all his eggs in the American educational basket.

Oscar kept coming to class even after he'd passed all his placement exams and submitted his high school applications. It was almost summer by then, and I didn't much feel like teaching. We'd sit around the classroom, watching movies about American high school students— highly stylized accounts, I told him, of the life he'd soon be leading. Oscar liked *Dead Poets Society*, but didn't care much for *Boyhood* (too long and too Southern). After these screenings, I'd ask him to write a short essay analyzing the underlying themes of each film. "X has an important message to share," these essays all began, and somehow, the message was always the same: "It takes great courage to get what you want from your life."

I didn't really know what Oscar wanted from his life—whether he'd try and stay in America, like my parents had, or come back to China, like most of his peers. I told my coworkers that Oscar was the most Westernized Chinese student I'd ever taught, a label we expats—people who'd gone to great lengths to get out of the West— somehow meant as a compliment. We all assumed that success abroad and acting Chinese were inversely related for our students. Aspiring to one meant dispensing, to some degree, with the other. And who better than the assimilated American Chinese guy to teach Oscar how to dilute his Chineseness, to write "critically" and perform as an individual, to talk and eat and maybe even think like an American, to quickly and quietly earn his degrees?

One might argue that a similar math applies to Americans trying to make it abroad, and yet in most parts of the world, following a local way of life is associated with tradition and even backwardness, while familiarity with America and its cultural products signals one's openness to the world. I didn't make these scripts, but I have followed them. It would be overstating many facts, that is, to say I taught Oscar how to be a cosmopolitan, unless it's also true that the best world citizens are those of us who can successfully pass as American.

> Unfortunately, cosmopolitanism has been reconstructed from such a variety of standpoints as to often confuse rather than clarify political-economic and cultural-scientific agendas. It has acquired so many nuances and meanings as to make it impossible to identify any central current of thinking and theorizing, apart from a generalized opposition to the supposed parochialisms that derive from extreme allegiances to nation, race, ethnicity, and religious identity.
>
> —DAVID HARVEY

BACK IN THE NINETEENTH CENTURY, CHINESE MIGRANTS IN the Americas were often referred to by Westerners as "celestials." The term was not intended as a compliment, but as a reminder of the Chinamen's origins in a mythic "Celestial Empire" in the East. As far as anti-Asian slurs go, I much prefer "celestial" to its historical descendants. A celestial sounds like a star-person, a space traveler not unlike a cosmopolitan. From way up there in the heavens, a celestial watches the world below.

In Chengdu, I, too, felt like I was floating above the city. Every day began and ended for me in Manhattan 2, with L spooning up behind me and those glorious windows at our fronts. We would lie there for hours, neither fully asleep nor awake, like mannequins stored behind glass.

In Chengdu, I told myself to write but always wound up at the mall instead, trying on mock-neck sweaters at Uniqlo. There were many malls in the city, and one of the largest was called Global Center. It had a Burberry, an InterContinental Hotel, and a Godiva Chocolatier; it had sushi restaurants, day cares, an indoor water park with a wave pool and slides. I was always at some point-of-sale in those days, flashing my WeChat pay code to the scanner.

In Chengdu, I went to see all the latest American films at the theater: *Star Wars: The Last Jedi*; *Blade Runner 2049*; *Black Panther*; *Jurassic World: Fallen Kingdom*; *Avengers: Endgame*; *Solo: A Star Wars Story*; *Thor: Ragnarok*; *Incredibles 2*. All the Hollywood tentpoles that year, and every year since, portrayed extraterrestrial or postapocalyptic worlds. With the notable exception of *Black Panther*, all of them starred white actors at the helm of multicultural casts. In other words, they were cosmopolitan films produced for cosmopolitan times. Because I saw them in China, I could also rest assured that they'd been vetted by a team of unseen censors. These censors were notoriously persnickety, alert to even the barest suggestion of anti-Chinese bias. An action flick from 2006—*Mission: Impossible III*, starring Tom Cruise—had run afoul of the censors by including a chase scene through Shanghai that featured laundry drying on metal racks outside apartment windows, a common enough sight in Chinese cities, but one not in keeping with the country's newly developed, laundry-less image.

In Chengdu, I read books by André Aciman, Walter Benjamin, Jorie Graham, Aleksandar Hemon, Yiyun Li, Teju Cole, Jess Row, T. S. Eliot, Chris Kraus, Du Fu, Jenny Zhang, Jenny Xie, Zadie

Smith, Elif Batuman, Audre Lorde, John Hersey, Roland Barthes—cosmopolitans, all.

In Chengdu, I listened to music made by the local band du jour: the Higher Brothers, a foursome of tatted-up rappers whose biggest hit was about how everything, everywhere was "Made in China." The Brothers took their moniker from the Chinese appliance maker Haier, a company that uses a pair of Speedo-clad robots—one blond and white, the other black-haired and Asian—as its mascots. These cheerful boy wonders can be seen embracing on many a Haier-made appliance, including the air conditioner above my Manhattan 2 bed. They'd even starred in their own animated television show back in the nineties. On that show, the brothers traveled together to five continents and fifty-six countries, learning about foreign places and people while trying to save the world from ecological disaster.

In Chengdu, I had this constant, low-grade worry that L would get lost somewhere in the East, and that I would never see him again. What these worries turned into was a lot of helicoptering on my part. For a year, I rarely let my blond-haired Haier Brother out of my sight. When we fucked, my fingers would splay on the rose-printed wallpaper above our headboard, a mauve expanse scripted all over with the French word for love, *l'amour*. Sometimes, our *amour*-making would be like a gentle girdling of stems. Other times, we'd enter a roiling rhythm, my hands probing for clandestine anthers and sticky stigmas, his chin notched into my shoulder as my feet flexed on his calves, all our horticultural parts pollinating each other at once, me and the wallpaper and L.

In Chengdu, I was always looking for some reprieve from all that vapor and smog. Once, I took L to a nearby holy mountain, hoping he'd see that China, too, had views. We climbed to the top, only to find that a sea of clouds had enshrouded the mountain's peak. Pretend there's an open sky in front of you, I said to him, recounting a composite collection of memories from long ago: all the different times I'd gone to a temple and done whatever it is Chinese people do in such spaces when they aren't religious but feel drawn into the orbit of "culture." Pretend that all the clouds are level below you, and that you're standing here with your mother and her parents, watching a murder of crows fly in and out of that sea. Maybe my grandparents had been spry enough back then to complete at least part of the climb. Maybe my mother walked at their pace as I raced ahead up the stairs. At the top, I stood before the Puxian Bodhisattva's golden statue, its ten faces that look in every direction at once. When my grandmother finally got to the summit, she had us write down our wishes on slips of paper. Instead of handing mine to a monk to be burned, as Apo instructed, I snuck my slip of paper outside to the viewpoint and gave my wish up to the wind.

In Chengdu, I eventually lost track of my backstory, my wants. Was I an aggrieved American sheltering abroad? A diasporic Chinese recalled to the mother ship? The reality is I was many things: a fretful boyfriend and lazy teacher, an aficionado of Chinese malls, a black-and-gray-clad presence at Kristen's late-night sets, a cheerless expat and writer of shitty poems. And all of that was okay, all of that contributed in small and big ways to the cumulative head rush of that year.

> Hopes that cannot be confined within the borders of a national culture are idle wishes: castles in the air.
>
> —PAUL GILROY

WHAT I HAVE BEEN ATTEMPTING TO DIAGNOSE IS MAYBE JUST the seamlessness of that time and that place, how Chengdu flowed, quicksilver and plastic, all around me, how my experiences in that place were all, in some way, inert, flattened into sheets made from the mind's gauziest materials. To say it bluntly, I did not feel like I was actually living there, and this seemed like both a Chengdu problem and a me problem, a misalignment between person and world.

About the time I started thinking of leaving Chengdu, I went, as one does, to get a new tattoo. My first tattoo had been, if not a mistake, then a happy stupidity. In Nashville, one summer, tipsy off a few mojitos, I'd asked a man in a Def Leppard tee to stencil a wire clothes hanger onto my clavicle. This time, I wanted something with more gravitas, something that might operate as a screen capture of my time in Chengdu. I brought the artist a panel from *The Whole Earth Catalog*, a compilation of Hokusai's early *edehon* drawings, and asked for a tattoo on my arm imbued with a similar feeling. Hokusai's drawings and woodcuts are known for representing Japan's "floating world" of ephemeral pleasures. The specific drawing I'd selected showed a traveler in a shallow stream, walking against the current. I told the artist I wanted a clean, rectangular border around my tattoo, just like in the *Catalog*. The artist warned me this might break the "flow" of the piece. I told him that was precisely the point.

When the tattoo was finished, L and I wandered over to Wenshu Monastery. We walked past the main building and into a garden studded with pools enclosed in massive stone basins, each with an island at its center and lily pads strewn on the water. This was one of our favorite places to go in Chengdu. It was easy to imagine each cistern as a world apart, set aside for the baby turtles perched on slimy roots, the mosquito larvae siphoning down air from above, the minnows darting as quickly as vision itself through flooded canals in the rock. In a way, L and I occupied our own island, our own world within a world. We noticed on each other's behalf when the gingkos on our block turned golden and shed their leaves. We reminded each other to drink water and call our respective parents. My assumption that I'd be the native informant and he my foreigner charge never really panned out. It was L who told me to breathe when I got that abscess in my mouth; who fished my to-do lists from the trash because he said we'd want to know what we'd done with all these days; who helped get us to every unheard-of destination I proposed (a park full of trash called Phoenix Mountain, a bookstore downtown with amphitheater-like seating, a field of flowering rapeseed where a missile factory once rose); who pretended not to notice when the waiters responded very slowly to my unpracticed Chinese; who cared enough to keep floating beside me in all that sculptural air, a celestial just like me.

Cosmopolitanism is supposed to teach us how to navigate the endlessly complex world that we have, and yet many of its advocates seem more adept at summoning alternative worlds than reckoning with our own. Living in China, I was always reading about the latest plans for some "high-tech," "sustainable," "innovative" development which was sure to break the mold of urbanism as we knew it. The late architect Zaha Hadid's firm recently broke ground outside Chengdu on a start-up village called Unicorn Island, which, when finished, will "foster the continued growth of China's digital economy, creating living and working environments for Chinese and international companies." Not to be outdone, Rem Koolhaas's Office for Metropolitan Architecture has proposed a master plan for the Chengdu Future Science and Technology City—a Broadacre-like concept divided into six integrated clusters ("agriculture," "energy," "sci-park," "recycling," "nursery," and "university"), all connected by a "smart mobility network" of driverless cars. As Julie Sze writes in *Fantasy Islands*, many such outposts of the future have already been erected in China, and exactly zero of them have turned out as promised. Like many of us now living on an Earth ironically in need of terraforming, I get the escapist appeal of such utopian demimondes. I also get that, unlike our Earth, worlds within a world usually end.

You can't fight fire with air.

—ZADIE SMITH

NO LONGER SURE WHAT I WAS DOING IN CHENGDU, I FOLLOWED my apo's instructions. I applied to graduate school—to PhD programs in American Studies, no less—and accepted an offer that spring. By summer of 2018, L and I had quit our jobs and begun planning an autumn return to the States. We changed the HEPA filter on our air purifier, the foam stained sooty and black, and carted the contraption up to my grandparents' apartment. Everything else we put on the side of New Hope Road so that the residents of Manhattan 2 could pick out what they wanted.

With not even the pretense of work to keep us in Chengdu anymore, L and I took a trip to Langmusi, a picturesque town on the Sichuan–Gansu border. I booked us onto a two-day horseback tour of the countryside—a bold choice, seeing as neither of us had ever ridden. The Tibetan teenager who was our tour guide never said a word to us, but the horses knew where they were going, and besides, that green yonder needed little explication. We spent the first day blissed out on pastoral scenery, and the first night sleeping in a one-room hut, cheek by jowl with a pair of yak herders whose relationship to our guide was difficult to ascertain. After a hearty dinner of yak sirloin over *mian pian*, we all settled down in front of a tiny television to watch the nightly newscast. The CCTV anchors happened to be discussing an escalating migrant crisis on the US–Mexico border. Their main visual aid was a now-infamous photograph of a Honduran girl in a bright pink sweatshirt, crying inconsolably as an American border cop patted down her mom.

Our hosts wanted to know when we planned on going back to America, and we told them soon, in just a few weeks or so. They told us to be careful, and then they said, more to each other than to us, that China was so safe, and that this was the best thing about it. That night, it stormed, raindrops pinging off a corrugated tin roof.

What does the cosmopolitan say during conversations like this? Does he vehemently denounce the sight of children being separated from their mothers by officers of Earth's wealthiest nation? Or does he ask his Tibetan hosts pointed questions about their own relationship to the Chinese state, the invisible strings attached to their new television, the scholarships to college in Lanzhou being offered to their sons in exchange for obedience, or at least quietude? In theory, the cosmopolitan refuses any of the easy answers offered by nationalism. He abstains from picking a side, and indeed advocates conscientiously for the humanity of all parties: the Honduran migrants and the American border cop, the Chinese-Tibetan herders and the American-expat tourists; they're all of one stock, one kind, one worldliness.

I've always found it easy to find my way to the cosmopolitan position when people start pitting nations against each other, because it's a nice position to occupy, one that telegraphs its own aversion to quick-tempered hot takes. Problems emerge, however, when one tries to turn cosmo-theory into cosmo-politics, what Pheng Cheah and Bruce Robbins think of as an "actually existing cosmopolitanism." Politics, for better or worse, is about finding common cause with someone else. It's about picking a side and accepting that side's foibles—not carte blanche, of course, but for the sake of taking concrete steps toward a shared objective. The side one picks doesn't have to be that of a morally derelict nation, but it most definitely can't be that of a woozily abstract world. A person is well within their rights to be from everywhere, all at once, but they have to be accountable to at least some of those places.

The people sleeping in the hut that night were all citizens of the world, but they were also subjects of two nations at cross-purposes with one another. The more privileged ones could perhaps daydream and act to the contrary, but in the end, they, too, had to acknowledge the nation they had come from, and could always return to, in a pinch. "Are they really so cruel, those Americans?" my hosts asked me in Chinese, our only shared language. The cosmopolitan that I am said nothing. He shut his mouth. He slept.

> It is only a right of temporary sojourn, a right to associate, which all men have. They have it by virtue of their common posses-sion of the surface of the Earth, where, as a globe, they cannot infinitely disperse and hence must finally tolerate the presence of each other.

—IMMANUEL KANT

THAT SPRING, THE NATIONAL PEOPLE'S CONGRESS VOTED ALMOST unanimously to suspend Xi Jinping's term limits as president, a move that my own country's president hailed as "great." America and China's usual state of equilibrium—one bought by economic codependence—was starting to unravel, with tariffs levied on Chinese solar panels and American soybeans. The years since have only continued that trend. Visas have been revoked, journalists expelled, classified documents thrown in open fires outside consulates in Houston and Chengdu. Less than two years after I left China for the last time, a pandemic began in Wuhan, before spreading to my own country-of-origin, and though this scourge posed what seemed to many like the epitome of a cosmopolitan problem, both China and America responded by doubling down on their nationalism and fingering the other as the culprit. The very job I had in Chengdu, glorified English tutoring, has since been effectively banned as part of a larger effort to reform public education and root out Western influences. Students like Oscar have stopped coming to America in such droves, though come they still do, and all the people I knew who used to teach those students, my former boss included, have gone back to their countries of origin.

I came to Chengdu not knowing that a time of cosmopolitan dreaming was coming to an end—not just for me, but for so many other transplants and expatriates. Now that I've left China, and don't know when I may return, I feel more chagrin than ever about how easily I took my time there for granted. That's the thing about cosmopolitanism: it bamboozles you into thinking that the world's interconnectedness will always win out; that borders may shut, but only for so long. And in the meantime, you never actually feel like you're living in Chengdu, or Bangkok, or Paris, because to really be in a place, you have to recognize you might lose it.

So, what did I lose, in leaving Chengdu? Nothing specific, which is perhaps the banal tragedy of it all. What's most galling to me now is that I came to Chengdu already having ties to that place, attachments I didn't nurture because I was stuck in the mindset of the cosmonaut who figured he'd always be back. After China sealed its borders to foreigners in 2020, all I could do was reminisce about my grandparents' blue-curtained apartment just outside the first ring, how every summer as a child I'd come to rest beside Apo on the couch while Agong went out to buy a few *youtiao* and Mom rubbed menthol ointment on my mosquito-bitten arms. Mom and Apo would be jabbering in a dialect I didn't understand, and the television would be on, though no one paid it any mind, and from these days of rain outside and doldrums within, I decanted an idea of what it means to live in a familial place, an idea about how time can actually be taught to stop in certain rooms with certain people, because a few years would pass and still the apartment sat unchanged, with me reading *Harry Potter* by the window as Apo and Mom kept chatting and Agong snuck a cigarette by the pungent hole in the bathroom, and later, we'd all walk together to a park by the Fu River, where I'd run through my wushu routines, jumping and circling, and the sweat would collect in the folds of my clothes, only to be pulled out later by the soapy water of that pink plastic basin that helps me remember the floor between Apo's feet, and she'd finish the laundry the next day, still talking to Mom, who was in the other room, chopping leeks and squashing roaches, and when this was done, Agong would ask me, because my arms were finally long enough, to hang the clothes out on the metal bars that jutted out from the window of their apartment, and I would do this using a kind of hook on a long metal pole, hoisting the still-wet clothes out through the window and into the open air, where the garments would fall into the line set for them by gravity and the tentative, chess-like movements of my pole: wet clothes clinging to wire hangers that somehow never let them go.

> Which would you rather your head be full of, facts or ideas?
> (Clouds, riposted the cosmopolitan.)
>
> —DONNA STONECIPHER

SOME YEARS AGO, KRISTEN INVITED ME TO AN ELECTRONIC music festival called Neverland. The festival was held at a place called

Xiannu Shan (仙女山), or Fairy Mountain. The music began on Friday afternoon and didn't stop until Sunday, at dawn, when all of us packed up our tents and went down the mountain to sleep.

At Neverland, there was no army of staff to disperse the mosh, no official sponsors, not even a printed schedule. I saw some beer kegs set up beside the dance floor, which was really just a muddy field, and a few tanks filled with nitrous. People from all over the world had come here to move their bodies in accordance with the festival's weekend-long song, our collective style a mishmash of jeweled headdresses, Disney cosplay, and Premier League kits. When the clouds started rolling, actually rolling, up the slope and over the stage, I thought of it as nature's fog machine and kept dancing. Laser lights diffused in the mist. Mud splatter Rorschached my torso. Every now and then, an opening would appear in the cloud cover, revealing balsa-wood kites constructed to look like dragons, their bodies connected by invisible cords to some dancer far below.

As a theory for how to live, cosmopolitanism no longer appeals to me, but I know the cosmos when it hits me over the head. Circling Neverland that weekend, I felt unabashedly connected to Earth and all its people, filled to the brim with that free-floating love that is the cliché of raves the world over, and yet a genuine upwelling of emotion nonetheless. Appiah observes that "cosmopolitanism is the name not of the solution but of the challenge." The challenge, as I've known it, is to figure out how to prolong this feeling for more than one weekend, until the everythingness of the world comes to permeate one's being. Such a cosmopolitanism may in fact be unattainable except in the most temporary of times under the most serendipitous of conditions. All I'm saying is that it happens, that cosmic feeling, and in its aftermath, we are changed.

Near the festival's end, a group of us gathered by Kristen's tent, where she introduced us to a driver she'd hired to take us down the mountain at precisely 3 a.m. Afterward, Kristen handed out the last bits of ecstasy stowed in her pack. We crushed the pills into our water bottles and drank.

Out on the mountain, cushioned by clouds on all sides, I felt the wind blow over and through me. I threw one tail of my scarf over my shoulder and danced with both utmost focus and perfect abandon. There was the notion, I'm sure, that we'd soon come down from this height, that we'd all pile into the driver's van and he'd take us away from Neverland and into the valley's dense and omniscient heat, and that some of us might spend years running around, trying to reclaim this overwhelming sensation, or at least trying not to forget how universally different we'd once seemed in each other's company. Sphingid hawk moths were flying out of the woods toward the dance floor, dusky brown shapes drawn to the flashing lights. I watched the giant moths frantically dive-bombing the stage, plunged into this ritual that nothing in their evolutionary history could've prepared them for, and for a moment, dancing in that sodden grass on top of Fairy Mountain, next to a friend of a friend and a Chinese girl in patent leather having the time of her life, I knew exactly how they felt.

TENNESSEE RIVER, 2013

Phenomenology of a Fall

B efore I remember falling, I remember watching it happen. I'm lying on my back in the grass as the trees shed their leaves above me. It's like a slow-motion scene in a film, or one of those backlit displays you often find in American Chinese restaurants, the kind that show mountains and waterfalls suffused with this oozing, dribbly light. The leaves fall from the tree, and my eyes track their progress, which isn't as linear as the story of Newton's apple foretells, embellished with many cartwheeling turns and sudden reversals, every leaf's flight path differentially affected by unseen forces above. But eventually, they all fall, landing around me in the yard with the crabapples and the long-legged wasps, the leaves' edges bruised and fragile, their veins rouged in gold.

When I was eight or nine, I joined the East Tennessee Wushu Team. One of the first lessons my *shifu* tried to teach us was how to properly fall. This involved flinging myself on the ground, trying always to lead with one shoulder, while using my other hand to guide the body's downward momentum into a tight roll that, if everything went well, would return me to the vertical plane. Shifu would bark out "ready position" and we'd all go still—backs straight, shoulders relaxed, eyes looking dead ahead. He would say, "*Yi bei, zou!*" and we would take the fall, tucking into ourselves and then unfolding again, trying to get back to a ready position.

If going to wushu practice every Saturday taught me how to fall with predictability, like clockwork, then jumping off a cliff into a lake taught me how to fall with abandon: a reckless teen trying his luck. I took the latter lessons while in high school, hanging out with my friends at a place called Mizell Bluff.

Located not far from Tellico Dam, Mizell Bluff—or "the cliffs," as we called it—is one of those Southern places I thought I would never miss but now do. In summer, the bluff has an Arcadian feel to it. Where the woods thin, a collection of sandstone knuckles begins, clenched over the rope swings and lost tires, the dungarees with no legs, the bullet casings and chigger stumps and neatly compacted cans of Natural Light. Locals come here to jump, and so on any given day there is usually an airborne body in view, someone slim and young and often tattooed. My friends and I drove there whenever our quiet and prosperous suburb seemed either too much or too little. Up at the cliffs, we were that group of multiracial nerds from across the county line who brought JanSports full of sunscreen instead of Igloos stocked with beer. We would spread out our towels a few feet back from the cliffside, which was always packed, the women spilling forth from Wet Seal bikinis, the men riding low in limp trunks. The cliffs contained a few distinct levels, with the highest ledge rising to around fifty feet above the water. One of my friends, the captain of my wushu team, would leap from the highest cliff with his back to the river, completing a rapid series of flips before entering the water below. Another friend would inch cautiously to the edge before stepping off in a docile motion, like a dog flashing its belly.

Technique-wise, I was somewhere in between the bold and the timorous. My preferred method was to walk calmly to the edge and pause there with my arms dramatically outspread, counting one, two, three under my breath before I leapt. I liked taking my time at the edge, gazing at the lake's far shore rather than the blue-green water below, thinking through each fall like I was a phenomenologist tinkering with a theory.

Theory #1: Falling may be the state that all jumpers seek, but falling is not the same thing as jumping. To jump and then fall coordinates descent. It preempts the moment of surrender.

Theory #2: A life full of jumps, of intentional falls, is probably a good one. We savor the downstrokes most when we have a safety net there to catch us. Jumping from a cliff and always coming back for more is putting gravity in action, but also a kind of privilege.

Theory #3: If upward progress is a sentimental image I have built my life around, then so, too, is falling, descent, the leaves floating unfettered above the yard.

I don't go jumping from the cliffs anymore, but I can't forget those days of free fall. That rush, it stays with you—the way my chin would draw close to my chest in medias res, the way that sound waves seemed to stretch, the water approaching my feet like a fermata. You don't forget those impacts, either, the body penetrating different densities and temperatures of lake. It was like being born, or never dying. It was like jumping from a great height into very deep water and feeling surprised the body could feel that way: one moment so light, the next so solid.

The last time I jumped from the cliffs was in 2013, at the tail end of another summer. It was my father's fiftieth birthday, and my family was celebrating at a lake house not far from the cliffs. My old wushu captain was there, turning aerials off the dock. Another former teammate lazed with me on the wooden deck, our bodies beaded in lake water and sweat.

When the party was over, my friends piled into my car and I drove us to the cliffs. We arrived near dusk and jumped only a few times before settling down on the cliff's edge to rest. A man struck up a conversation with us. He told us that he'd grown up not far from here, in a town called Friendsville, and that he had a baby on the way with a woman he loved, but not in the forever kind of way. He told us that one of his dreams was to visit Japan, and he spoke of something car-related called the Japanese domestic market, which he used like an adjective, as in "my ride is JDM as fuck." He asked where we all were from, and we said something to the effect of China, to which he responded, "No shit."

At sunset, the man killed his beer and asked if we wanted to jump again. My friends and I politely refused. I remember diving, later, into the water, bubbles detaching in little search parties from my mouth. I remember one of my friends entering the water above me, the dull boom of his impact, the way a person can come into or out of a story.

And so it goes, you might say. A man decides to do something risky. He sees a gamble, one where the collateral is maybe his life, and he takes it. My fourth and final theory is that the collateral is the same for all of us. We make the same wager every day, in different ways and weighted by very different odds. Driving the car, taking a drag, kissing a man out on the street, boarding planes, writing and acting in dissent or solidarity or both. I want to know more people who would jump off a cliff just because their friends did, more people who'd want to fall through the world beside me, if only for a time.

In the part of the South where I grew up, a summer sunset lingers in the air. The light leaves this afterglow, a carbon copy of day. When the police arrived, my friends and I gave our statements and left, driving back home on the same roads we always took. We would read the next day of a man whose body had been found in the waters below Mizell Bluff.

I did not know that man—the life he led and all he left behind. But I know his last moments were backlit and swift. His is the image of falling I can't shake, its purest phenomenon, when being and nonbeing meet and switch places in the air. A man comes running up from behind me. He leaps over my head, spinning in midair to yell a good natured "fuck y'all" and give us the bird. There is no planning, no do-overs, no countdown at the edge. I hear a splash far below, and later, not much else.

NAGARKOT, 2015

The Figure a Trip Makes

II. THE HOUSE

After the trip ends, I try and recover all the beautiful whatevers. I return to the broken house on the hill and take many photographs of it: an open door, a floor of sand, the white, flowering weeds that wend their way through tears in the windows' mesh. The house is just one room enclosed by gray stone on four sides. Whatever roof there once was has rotted away, the house's interior exposed to the elements. The front door stands much as I left it, ajar, an invitation to leave as much as to enter. I enter the house, but keep the door open.

A Jesuit missionary named Matteo Ricci once tried to teach the Chinese how to remember. In his *Treatise on the Mnemonic Arts*, written in Chinese, Ricci left instructions for how to build a memory palace, a structure for organizing the mind's wayward contents. One starts by visualizing a space: for instance, a house. The palace builder then furnishes his creation with objects and images, each of which shall serve as the anchor point for a memory. These tenterhooks must be arranged in an unbreakable series, so that every time one enters the palace, they find their recollections exactly where they left them. Ricci writes, "Once your places are all fixed in order, then you can walk through the door and make your start."

I walk around the house, trying to place its contents in order, and to graft upon each a moment from my travels. In one corner, I see a lighter half-buried in the sand, which I connect to a memory from yesterday, *lying with Josh in the leaf litter, amidst the Himalayan drift.* I link the house's open entrance to the long hike that brought us here, *walking on the dirt path out of Chisapani, a pack of local dogs graciously showing the way;* the metal girders propped against one wall to the city we'd recently exited, *the crowds filtering in and out of Durbar Square.* When I've filled the house with as many memories as I can, when I have turned it into my trip's palace, I head back to the hotel and pack my things.

It's April in Nepal, bees and butterflies fumbling in the springtime air. My friend Josh and I wait in the center of town for a van to arrive. It will come to us in a sputtering of exhaust, crowded already with men bound for Kathmandu. The van will pass through the valley, and the valley will fill it with more men, and when we come together to the city limits, we will disembark on a street corner under a red awning emblazoned with the word *Coca-Cola*, and my trip, as ever, will go on.

"What were you doing back there in the house?" Josh asks me.

"Trying to remember."

AFTER THE TRIP ENDS, I CIRCLE BACK TO WHERE IT BEGAN. I return to my parents' house, to Knoxville, to Tennessee. It's like I cannot convince my brain that a period of transience and travel has ceased until I remind it of its initial environs. In this way and others, I am a creature of sentiment, and of habit.

In 2015, at the end of my year-long journey through Asia, I get off the plane in Boston and make a beeline for the Chinatown bus. I'm in New York for what feels like a beat, then Baltimore, then DC. When I arrive in Knoxville, my parents pick me up at the Greyhound station downtown. They shuttle me to their new house in the suburbs, which has all the same furniture but not the same bones as the house I grew up in. The new house is one neighborhood over from the old house. It is basically an expansion of that earlier residence, with one additional floor—the basement—and a room outfitted for guests downstairs. Much like the old house did, this house sits on a hill, though much closer to the hill's summit than before.

I'm not sure if it's the house's fault, or jet lag's, but for several nights, I cannot sleep. I stay up late in the room where my parents have deposited my childhood effects, watching *Grey's Anatomy* and writing emails to friends. One of these emails declares, "I am an ongoing error in proprioception," as if the trip has refused to "let me go." It is easy to be melodramatic when you are a full-grown adult living again, however briefly, beneath your parents' roof—easy, too, to fall into old journals and memories, one's bottomless nostalgia for what has passed.

In the neighborhood where I grew up, there was just one long road leading up a hill, with cul-de-sacs jutting off on both sides. Developers in my town lay the roads down first before penciling in each lot. To the landscape historian J. B. Jackson's question of "Which came first, the house or the road leading to the house?" people where I'm from believe the road is always the answer. Each of our neighborhoods begins this way: as an asphalt diagram branded onto the land, black and dense and full of fumes.

My family lived near the base of the hill, in a redbrick house appointed with all the usual suburban amenities: a fenced backyard, a three-car garage, a chimney (purely decorative), and a light screening of trees out front. The running back of my high school football team lived near the top of the hill. His house looked like ours, only grander and with two stone lions guarding its front. Every day, he'd get on the bus at its penultimate stop, not looking at me or anyone really, and we'd all go to school that way, us kids from the Ridge, and over the years we did only the usual damage to each other, the usual names and phrases, and eventually, the running back went on to Ole Miss on a sports scholarship, and received a DUI, and dropped out, and drove his Acura back home and straight into an early death. No one I knew from my neighborhood was surprised by this turn of events. We all remembered that time on the bus when the running back's sister stabbed him in the thigh with a No. 2 pencil, how he dealt her three walloping punches to the jaw in response. This brutal episode hove back into view after the running back's death, perhaps because we found it premonitory of his fate. According to one news report, the running back was ejected from his car when it skidded like a loose puck off the highway. He'd driven much too fast onto the on-ramp, with intentions of going west.

Call it the auguries of the suburbs, the stories that asphalt diagrams beget. Carried to term in that amniotic sac, us kids from the Ridge kept only the most protean of confidences. We heard tell of everything, and wasted no time in passing our notes: the secretary doctoring invoices to fund her daughter's Midsummer's Masque (an also-ran for MTV's *My Super Sweet Sixteen*); the musclebound algebra teacher caught canoodling with one of his comelier students; the cheerleader's gay best friend who crafted a red strapless dress entirely from the petaled remnants of Solo cups—a contrivance put on display in the school's cafeteria for the better part of a year—who even made it as far as Parsons, which is to say, out of our town, only to learn that out of our town was where he couldn't hack it. These stories all ended as most suburban parables do, with the secretary bolting for the border but getting apprehended in Apache Junction, the algebra teacher transferred up the ladder into admin, and the gay best friend working sales at Sunglass Hut, shilling frames and scrolling through Grindr on his break. They're minor fables, really, and yet I have names and faces for them all, maybe because my memory clings most fiercely to gossip, or maybe because all these stories started off inside the sacred radius of where I'm from, and so they, like me, are emanations of that place. I passed the notes on, I subscribed to their logic. That logic held that every house's near-identical facade concealed at least one identity on the brink, people whose dreams the neighborhood fed on, but also made possible in some respects, even as the dreamers sought only escape.

I'm not sure when I became one of those people: someone who wanted so badly to exceed the gravity of a single-family home on a cleared plot of land. For a long time, I did not want anything more than the houses on the hill, the yards and culverts and relict little groves that spread out alongside, a built environment turned over to child's play, to games. I've often struggled to describe the suburbs to people who haven't lived there before: how easy these places are to leave, how difficult they are to forget. Life there feels like a self-enclosed system, pegged to the simple dualities of inside and outside, day and night, homework and then play. Here on the hill, everything was cyclical, becalmed, and yet none of it had been here for long, and none of it had emerged as the offspring of chance.

As my father was fond of reminding me, a house in the American suburbs was not a birthright to him or my mother. He made sure I

knew he'd grown up differently, shoehorned into a minuscule apartment in Wenzhou he shared with his brother and my grandparents, an
apartment beside other apartments, where any visit to the bathroom
could turn into a humiliating, communal affair. His family's story, or
the one he told me, was that they'd once possessed both money and
land, but then some members of the family had been labeled intellec-
tuals, class traitors, and they'd lost it all to revolution, only to gain it
back in the reform years by dint of their unflappable perseverance. This
backstory seemed to explain a lot. It was how my immigrant father
managed to value both individual attainment and outward conformity
in equal parts, and why every piece of parental counsel he ever gave me
boiled down to the same adage-like advice: "Work hard, be normal."

My mother's family had no such mythology of loss and resurrec-
tion, but she, too, grew up in cramped and unsentimental spaces. The
first home she can remember was built completely from wood and
sited on an alleyway running perpendicular to Dongjiadu Road in
Shanghai. This house was split into many units, and my grandmother
rented one of them. No one ever locked their doors in that house, as
there was nothing of value to steal. My apo often watched a neighbor's
six children when their mother was away at work, and sometimes,
especially during winter, she'd let her favorite of the neighbor kids
sleep over in the apartment. Even when they weren't in the home itself,
the neighbors' voices carried through the walls. That is something
both my parents remark on when speaking of their childhood homes:
the complete absence of personal space, of privacy. Their recollections
remind me of Jackson's writing on the "vernacular home," which, in
contrast to the "jealously guarded territory" of a house in the American suburbs, is not kept separate from its surroundings—neither fully
public nor sealed off like a vault. Of course, this interpenetration of

private and public space carried a different, much less salutary valence in the China of my parents' upbringings. Under Mao's regime, private life itself was at times verboten, a mark of either Western influence or insufficient commitment to the Party and its cause. Family homes and domestic matters were not just shared with neighbors, but with the many eyes and ears of the state (many times, those eyes and ears belonged to one's family). A wall could never separate you from what was outside, for the outside was already within.

I think about this a lot: how my parents grew up without privacy, but then made a home in America in which privacy, for me, was a too-plentiful resource. Do our divergent images of home explain some of our other differences as well? My deeply entrenched desire to make my thoughts and feelings public versus their reticence about their private lives. The careful attention they pay to outward appearance, to facades instead of interiors.

Growing up in the suburbs, I spent an inordinate amount of time in my own head, and when I wasn't there, I was up at the top of the hill, exploring the houses still under construction. By middle school, I'd developed a fascination for these unfinished residences, skeletal frames of blond wood, sheeted in Tyvek house wrap, with glassless windows and screenless porches, gravel driveways, interior walls you could walk through, stairs without balustrades, Whirlpools shining white in the sawdust mire of an almost-bathroom, living rooms that soared like the insides of some European cathedral. The unoccupied rooms at each site offered me ample space for daydreaming. Who might grow up here when the property was finished and sold? Which nooks would be their favorites, which angles of light through which windows? What kinds of pain would they inflict on each other? What sorts of love?

I should note that a few of those sites are still there, still unfinished. A housing bubble burst in 2008, and the buyers all retracted
their offers. When I visit my parents today, I always go back to the top
of the hill and look at them, these ruins of buildings that never were.

Not long after the running back's death, I saw a quote from one of
his friends in our local newspaper. "I don't know where that fine line is
where you have meaningful conversation and you're not just catching
up with people," the friend remarked. "I don't know if you can develop
a formula for that. I don't know how you do that correctly every time."
Suburbs like the one I grew up in are like the stage sets for tales of
losing touch. One by one, we kids from the Ridge headed out: for
college, for the military, for sports franchises and cinema. Two major
interstates, I-40 and I-75, merge right outside my hometown. Every
kid I know who grew up on that hill also knows the sound of that
mega-highway, the low moan of so many trucks in flight. You might
say it was the sound beneath every other sound, the backing track to
the tinkling of wind chimes and the eagerly savored first expletives, a
frequency I used to tune into each night from my bed, when all in my
vicinity was still and silent, but in the distance, this rush.

AFTER THE TRIP ENDS, I CAN'T STAY STILL. HOME—THE SPATIAL
equivalent to an article of faith—does not ground me as it should. In
fact, my parents' new house seems to have an opposite, inciting effect.
Being inside it, sleepless, makes me feel manic, and eating even basic
food causes indigestion, sending me to the toilet for another watery,
ochered shit. Several days pass like this, with me cycling restlessly between couch and bed, trying to calm my racing thoughts with television and tea.

Half of Homer's *Odyssey* documents what happens on Odysseus's trip; the other half relates what happens after the traveler has already arrived, incognito, back in Ithaca. Homecoming is not an event but a process, an undertaking potentially as onerous as any trip. Coming home can be difficult because in so many aspects, traveling feels like the diametric opposite to home life. Travelers are people who have left their homes behind, who live in thrall to a different proposal: that they may be at home in the world instead. The houses a traveler stays in are mere depots and temporary holding patterns, the kind of affectless "machines for living" praised by Le Corbusier. Even if these physical structures are, for their proprietors, layered with meaningful memories, the traveler has not come to excavate those histories. Houses are, to him, the most gossamer of impressions, like the loose strands of a spider web playing across his cheek. The sojourner experiences space as a vessel emptied of the long-term and the iterative, as a map picked clean of place.

Such an affinity for emptiness should, theoretically, have served me well in all my trips to China. In the early twenty-first century, the country appeared to be obliterating itself at an ever-accelerating rate. Millions of Chinese families had migrated to the cities or entered the urban middle class, spurring the largest spate of construction in human history. To make something new, something old had to be cast out. All over China, any remotely old-looking building I came across was usually spray-painted with the word 拆, or "tear down." I saw a white yak lumbering through the cinders of old Shangri-La; dilapidated barns near Hailar and defunct zoos in Jinghong; old schools outside Songpan that farmers had repurposed into concrete chicken coops; apartment buildings in Xi'an whose tenants had left in a hurry, leaving behind piles of textbooks, floppy disks, a blue-eyed baby doll with teased-out hair. When I visited Shanghai in 2014, I found not even a word to mark where my mother's first home used to be; her alleyway, indeed the entire city block she used to live on, had already been cleared.

I tried my best to move with dispassion through all this, not just the old homes tagged for demolition, but the shimmering transit hubs, cavernous malls, and seemingly endless ranks of high-rise apartments that had risen up in their place, one vacancy succeeding another. (Although China has the highest home-ownership rate in the world, an estimated sixty-five million of the country's newly built houses stand unoccupied.) And yet I still felt drawn to the emptiness that collects in a space once intended to hold a family, the melancholia evoked by yesterday's unwanted houses, as well as today's. I wondered where memories go when deprived of a tether—when all that is left are the psychic timbers of a mental palace. I asked myself the most basic, but essential, of questions: Where is my home in the world? How will I know when I find it?

I carried only one book with me as I traveled: *The Poetics of Space* by Gaston Bachelard. In it, Bachelard tries to identify what he calls "images of *felicitous space*," images that impart a sense of home, reminding a person of the special eternity that gathers inside a beloved abode. Someone's home images are always pegged, Bachelard argues, to their memories of a "first house," the one that taught them how to live. "The house we were born in is more than an embodiment of home," he writes, "it is also an embodiment of dreams." This edifice is nothing short of the "original shell," one whose inside "has engraved within us the hierarchy of the various functions of inhabiting." The first house—its image—centers our being long after we've outgrown its material site.

"Now everything becomes clear, the house images move in both directions: they are in us as much as we are in them." Out in the world alone, freely wandering, I have read this line over and over.

AFTER THE TRIP ENDS, I TRY AND REBUILD THE HOUSE. PERHAPS this is the image of felicitous space most ingrained in me: the house one arrives at only after a long journey, the house generated by every trip. Odysseus's sole objective in *The Odyssey* is getting back to Ithaca. His road is the classical one, in that it points, after many deviations, to a home he used to know. My parents' trip has yet to turn back on itself in the same way, but it, too, produced a residence—the one to which I habitually return.

Now, like a visitor, I examine the product, the house and all its assembled accoutrements. The fridge three-fourths covered in magnets that say "Toronto," "Fort Lauderdale," "Yellowstone National Park." The aquarium with its dwindling population of goldfish. The Starbucks mugs sourced from all the countries visited by my father. The blue orchids prized by my mother. The pictures in their frames—most all of them of us. The research accolades and plaques placed on the living room shelf behind shifting piles of *Science*. The paper baskets my mother used to make to hold sunflower seed casings. The copious evidence of children who won spelling bees and participation medals. The colored-pencil rendering of our old house, drawn by my grandfather.

Another line I like from the *Poetics*: "The house, as I see it, is a sort of airy structure that moves about on the breath of time." Sometimes, I've learned, entire houses—not just their builders—can travel overseas. In Salem, Massachusetts, there is an eighteenth-century Chinese house called Yin Yu Tang on display at the Peabody Essex Museum. The house is not a reproduction, but an actual former residence that the museum relocated—brick for brick and beam for beam—from Huizhou village in Anhui Province. Back in its former footprint,

Yin Yu Tang was the "first house" of a wealthy merchant family, the Huangs. Up to thirty people from multiple generations had lived together inside the compound's sixteen rooms. In the late 1990s, a binational team of architects and preservationists deconstructed the entire structure and shipped it to Salem. The Chinese house was rebuilt in New England to model exactly what it had looked like in 1982, right before its abandonment—a meticulous act of cultural exchange. Visitors today can stand in the outer courtyard, where livestock once milled, and behold the house's stark white walls washed in lime stucco (a sun-reflecting design feature common in hot and humid Huizhou that has since outlived its original purpose). They can proceed from there into the inner courtyard, or *tianjing* (sky well), to look up into the same slim aperture of sky where Huang children gazed in Qing Dynasty times, and count the many goldfish stocking the two pools that used to catch rainwater from above. Yin Yu Tang's name is often translated as the "Hall of Plentiful Shelter."

Some houses come over from China; others are sent back. That is the story of the towers outside Kaiping, which I visited during my year abroad. In the mid-nineteenth through early twentieth centuries, young men from Kaiping migrated in droves to the United States, Canada, and parts of Southeast Asia. Their families used the remittances from these *huaqiao* to construct elaborate, columnar houses called *diaolou* in each family's ancestral village. With lawlessness on the rise in late Qing China, the *diaolou* were built as fortresses, but also as testaments to the wealth and good fortune of the families whose sons had gone away. The *diaolou*'s outsides, especially their tops, were decorated in an exuberant bricolage of oriental and occidental styles, with roofs shaped in that distinctively Chinese way and entrances inscribed overhead with characters, but also fortified ramparts adorned with Roman eagles surrounded by gilded acanthus leaf. Their interiors featured modern sewing machines and crates of Kentucky bourbon next to coromandel screens enclosing traditional family shrines.

I went to see the *diaolou* because I found their story irresistible in its pathos: overseas sons erecting fantastical towers to shelter families they'd left behind (houses some of these men would never get to see, stuck as they were in a gold mine or laundromat on the other side of the ocean). I imagined the men forming in their minds the image of a house, one suited to the cultural contact zones and transnational capitalist markets they operated within, and then their parents manifesting that image on the sacred grounds of the *laojia*. Today, no one lives in the *diaolou* anymore, and only a few of the more picturesque structures have been preserved for tourists. Children go into the decrepit buildings at night, the ones with overgrown turrets and mice-infested floors. They wander together or alone from room to room, playing games amongst themselves.

AFTER THE TRIP ENDS, I MUST TEAR DOWN THE HOUSE AGAIN. I am still awake, still not sleeping through the night. My mother tells me to stop thinking so much about it. The problem, she believes, is chronic. "You overthink everything; you've been this way since you were young."

Instead of sleeping, I quit my parents' house, padding in flip-flops across the overgrown lawn. My nocturnal walk feels furtive, even if my parents are long past caring what I do with my nights. When we lived in that other house, the house I'm headed to now, my brother and I often snuck out after dark, charting a well-worn path from our bedroom window across a low roof and down a trellis into the yard. I feel weirdly like I'm trying to find that path again, to worm my way back into that place where I learned my own "functions of inhabiting."

All through middle school, the boys in my neighborhood held in trust a copy of our school directory, inside of which we highlighted the addresses of all the kids whose houses we wanted to strike. We'd walk from our hill to neighborhoods two or three miles away, always diving into roadside ditches whenever a car sped past. We were ruthless on those nights, egging windows, forking lawns, uprooting flower beds, pissing on mailboxes, draping picket fences in graceless streamers of white. A Vietnam veteran named Don lived alone at the end of my cul-de-sac. I spent much of one autumn harassing him, mostly because a neighbor boy told me that Don liked to call my brother and me "little gooks" or something like that. Every time I snuck out, I made sure to ring Don's doorbell and then run. Once, I stole every issue of the *Farragut Press* off my neighborhood's driveways and stuffed them into his mailbox. On another occasion, I snapped twigs into tiny pieces and rigged them into coital skeletons on his stoop.

What comes into a child to align him against a house? A wildness, surely, or maybe a fearlessness birthed from boredom, unideological and fervid. Around the time I started this quiet war, I read a story by Graham Greene called "The Destructors," a story in which a band of boys targets an old man and his house. This house is tall and aristocratic-looking, but shabby inside, with a helical staircase corkscrewing down its middle. When the old man goes away on holiday, the boys break in, relieving the house of its fixtures, its floors, and its wiring. They unmake the house from the inside out, and they do this not out of spite, but reverence, for "destruction after all is a form of creation."

We kids from the Ridge never performed quite as comprehensive a demolition, and yet our petty vandalisms were still in service
to, I believe, a kind of negative creation. This was our way of making our little world fall apart, of turning ruination into an activity and a feat. I could cite teenage angst as our reason; I could talk
specifically about my Asianness and Don's whiteness, the righteous
fury of a queer and restless teen, but that wouldn't encompass all the
other stuff: the undeclared foreign wars being waged in our names,
the hand-wringing about trade deficits and 50 Cent, the mortgage-
backed securities being sold by deterritorialized banks, or how in a
few years all these illusory securities would make our bed and sleep in
it, royally fucking every house, and how none of it mattered because,
in the grand scheme of things, we were fine, we were golden, all of us
ingots cast from pyrite American dreams. I think it was all of that and
more: this primal urge to break something, to rage against the old on
behalf of the new. It was also all of that and less, much less.

Don eventually called the cops on me, and they paid a visit to our
house. My parents were too shocked to be angry. They hadn't known
until then that I had been sneaking out. "What got into you?" they
asked me, and I did not have an answer. How could I tell them something I barely knew myself? That the houses on the hill had started to
feel like those other ones to me, the structures abandoned before they
were even complete. I trudged over to Don's and rang his doorbell. I
apologized to the old man's feet.

AFTER THE TRIP ENDS, I CANNOT SAY WHAT HAPPENED TO THE
house. The structure is probably still standing, still functionally intact—it is home that became a moving target.

In April 2015, I went to Kathmandu just a few weeks before an earthquake ripped the city asunder. This is what I remember of that place: Chipped blue paint on a wall. Macaques extracting Frito-Lay tribute. A girl with flowers in her hair feeding the pigeons in Durbar Square. My calves hooked around the neck of a plastic surgeon from Miami, this tiny dream catcher dangling from his chest.

I can't accurately say how much time I spent in Kathmandu. It felt like a long weekend, maybe two. I know because I wrote down that the taxi from Tribhuvan Airport to downtown cost eight hundred rupees, and that my friend Josh booked us a room at a hostel called the Sparkling Turtle. I know that we spent most of the ensuing days in the backpackers' ghetto of Thamel, specifically in that maze of streets near Or2k, a vegetarian Israeli restaurant, and the Café Himalaya. I know that at some point Josh attended the largest Passover seder outside of Israel, and that at another point, there was a bandh called by the Maoists that brought the whole city to a halt. I know that I took 3,672 photographs in Kathmandu, each an image for my palace: Bob Marley bumper stickers, goji berries wrapped in a child's math homework, signs reading "DEAR HUMAN PLEASE TOUCH ME" and "IF I HAD A HAMMER, I'D SMASH WHITE SUPREMACIST CAPITALIST PATRIARCHY."

One morning in Kathmandu, Josh and I decided to hike to Nagarkot, a hill resort where the Nepalese royal family used to summer. The trail snaked along terraced valleys and up a few minor mountains, its edges trimmed in red rhododendron and the fiddleheads of ferns. As we walked, we talked, picking up the strand of a conversation we'd begun years ago in college. Our patter touched on the writers we most venerated at the time—A. R. Ammons, C. P. Cavafy, and Loren Eiseley—the destinations we'd crossed off our lists since last we'd seen each other, the close calls with shot girls in Tbilisi and Jeepneys in Manila, and all the people back in America we still somehow held in common. By our conversation's end, we'd arrived in Nagarkot and could see snowcapped mountains from our room at the New Dragon Hotel.

Our plan for what to do in Nagarkot was simple. The next day, Josh and I each placed a tab of acid on our tongue and went for a walk in the woods. The forest was placid, unremarkable, and then it was something flowy and entropic, a series of textured ducts we passed through, running. Grasshoppers wowed us with flashes of their red and black underwings. A vulture hovered overhead for several minutes as we sat, stupefied, on a terrace far below. After making a circuit of the village, and reading each other choice passages from Whitman, Josh and I came to a broken house on top of a hill. We pushed through the house's front doors and walked into a space overgrown with flowering weeds. The empty house had just one room, with a fire circle at its center. A large mammal had recently defecated inside the circle, and white butterflies were inspecting the excrement. Angular rays of sunlight illuminated the house and all its manifold contents. We scaled one of its walls and sat there, looking down at an image of felicitous space.

In my brain agog on acid, I knew I'd been here before, knew it more surely than I'd ever known anything else. I had returned, somehow, to the house my parents had made for me on that hill. In fact, I'd never left that house, not fully, even as my comings and goings had punched holes in all its walls. The first house was still first. All my traveling would never take me too far away from it, nor caulk and buttress its walls. It would stay inside me, this perfect wreck of a thing, lacking in any distinction and yet pellucid in its depths, a face held open to the sky.

———

AFTER THE TRIP ENDS, I TRY ONE LAST TIME TO COME BACK. When I finally lay eyes on it, that house on the hill is how I figured it would be: here, but also gone. The buildings we know as children shrink as we age, contracting as one's point of view expands, but looking at the house now, I can tell its basic substance is the same. I used to live here, I think to myself, lurking awkwardly at the property's edge. I used to sit on that blue swing whose chain has finally been mended, used to sneak out of that window to scamper across the roof and dangle my legs over the gutter until my bare feet grazed the wood and I could step down into the night.

"I still remember it," my mother once told me. She is walking again through the door of her first house, the one just off the alleyway in Shanghai. There is a small annex downstairs where all the cooking and washing takes place, and to her left, a stairway leading up into the attic. So many years have passed since there was even a threshold there to cross, and yet the memory palace stays intact.

Josef Brodsky writes, in an essay titled "In a Room and a Half," about growing up in such a space. As a child, he used to want nothing more than to leave his parents' side, to be out there, "into the wide world." That child "gets his wish." He crafts a new house in a new country for himself, a reality separate from the one that came before, and while he is hard at work mastering this new reality, the old one is fading, as realities do. One day, Brodsky notices that the house that raised him is no longer there. "On that day he feels like an effect suddenly without its cause."

The house, the diagram, the construction sites left unfinished— they're all still here, all still waiting. Unlike Brodsky, if I wanted to recreate this life for myself, I probably could, but reprising the suburbs would not return me to that time when the cause was still close at hand, when I could live so happily cloistered on that isthmus of the mind where everything was real and not yet a reference to everything else. The departure from such a place can't be reversed. I left my house, touched its walls, smelled my fingers, lay on the bare carpet that last summer day as grass grew an easy inch in our yard. Things go, or so you let them. A person comes up in a small place so they may know the beatitude of escape. They relish it, that leave-taking, until they can't anymore. Now they've fallen like crabapples into the street again, the kind that bruise underfoot. Or they're like me on my rollerblades, coming down the hill that one time, the road a passageway down through the green, always wanting to go the whole way and even further, but then pitching sideways across the curb because I knew, in the end, I couldn't. This is the kind of ambiguous loss that follows me time after time, place after place: when you've been on your way out for as long as you can remember, but then, Orpheus-like, you look back, and it's gone. Or not *gone* exactly, but ruined, and you don't know how that happened, or why you needed to come down from that hill.

NAGARKOT, 2015

What the River Gave Me

I. PATTERN

Every day I go down to a river, mostly to walk or run beside it, but sometimes just to stand and look at the water. Water flowing down a channel is like sand in an hourglass—matter measuring time. But the sand never stops, not in my years beside rivers, not yet. "Eventually, all things merge into one, and a river runs through it," writes Norman Maclean. The river, like time, always outlasts its keepers.

I first read Maclean's *A River Runs through It* in college, which was also the first time I lived by the river I look at today. The river is called Charles, after the English king. I once wrote a paper dedicated to the Charles for a class I was taking on the literatures of place. For that class, I also read William Carlos Williams's *Paterson*, a book-length poem about a city in New Jersey that heavily influenced my understanding of the relationship between rivers and lives. The book's structure mirrors that of a river, one modeled after the Passaic, which still runs through Paterson today:

From the beginning I decided there would be four books following the course of the river whose life seemed more and more to resemble my own life as I more and more thought of it: the river above the Falls, the catastrophe of the Falls itself, the river below the Falls and the entrance at the end into the great sea.

I devoted most of my paper to analyzing the poetry of Williams and a few other river-obsessed Western writers; my interest in rivers, though, was far more personal than hermeneutic. I found the seeming equivalence between a human's life—mine in particular—and a river's both accurate and alluring. What other feature of landscape could so elegantly embody the meandering course of biography—a life's intermittent changes in speed and location, its inundating, relentless progress? To hydrologists, every river can be divided into the same basic sequence of headwaters, upper course, middle course, lower course, and mouth. Considering one's life in riverine terms thus imposes a linear pattern on what can often feel like disconnected parts. Positioned rather close to my headwaters back then, with little notion of what lay ahead, I thrilled to the idea of a format proposed by nature, a pattern animated by constant movement and yet funneled in one direction. I began to identify with the rivers I knew—Tennessee and Charles, Yangtze and Huangpu—and to bring myself to their banks. One byproduct of such thinking is the assumption that understanding a river will, by transitive property, elucidate some aspects of life.

II. COMPANIONSHIP

There used to be a river that ran about a mile north of where I grew up. This river had no name, or none that I'd been told; it was a skimpy, maundering thing, really more of a creek than a river. Getting there involved cutting through several backyards, crawling beneath a barbed wire fence, and finally descending into a wooded dell through which the water moved, at turns sluggish and swift.

I was almost ten years old when I first came to the water—old enough, in America at least, to already believe this side of the world had once been "New" and all its places undiscovered. Maybe this was such a place, and if so, why not claim it? I surveyed the river's pebbly banks and splashed through its pools. I turned over rocks, looking for crayfish and salamanders. As the river's different sections became more known to me, I chose for them borrowed names. The river's one little cascade I of course named "Niagara Falls." A wider stretch where the water trickled over tree roots I dubbed the "Spanish Steps." With no evidence to the contrary, I thought of the river as a place only I cared for or knew. My river ran in the crease between two hills, on a rolling expanse of cow pasture, not far from a field I also used to haunt. But the river was more to me than a territory; it was a calming, talkative presence. The river was always going somewhere, following its own path of least resistance. I liked watching it happen—the river, its rivering—while sitting on a fallen tree trunk over the channel, one hand touching the water's surface as tadpoles slipped skins in the shallows and day whittled down into dusk. I asked myself where the river came from, and every visit thereafter ended with an effort to locate its mysterious source, the answer always obscured by thickets of poison ivy and thorn.

III. FAMILY

I don't know how to relate to people who do not also relate to rivers. My mother grew up beside two tributaries of the Yangtze—also known as the Changjiang, or "Long River." My father was born by a shorter river called the Oujiang, in Wenzhou, and my brother is named, in Chinese, for that industrial waterway. If people know of Wenzhou, they know it for its famously complex dialect, which is mutually unintelligible with Mandarin. The dialect is so incomprehensible to outsiders that the Chinese military used Wenzhounese to formulate codes during World War II. My father's dialect is sometimes referred to as the "Devil's Language," and sometimes as *"ouyu,"* or the language of the river. I have never learned to speak it.

IV. CONTROL

I grew up in the Tennessee River Valley, a landform shaped by water's retention and flow. What we called the river behaved in most stretches like a lake, and it behaved that way because of the dams—nine on the Tennessee's main drag alone—that metered the river's height and regulated its moods.

Before the dams' construction, the Tennessee Valley had been blighted by poverty and flooding. It was the arrival of the great dam builders, the TVA (Tennessee Valley Authority), that changed all this. Established in 1933, the TVA was the only New Deal program tasked with the management and rehabilitation of one specific region. President Roosevelt described it as a "corporation clothed with the power of government" and "one of the great social and economic achievements of the United States." Upon visiting the dams thirty years later, President Kennedy declared that "the initials TVA stand for progress." The federal government's promise to my valley's people had been simple: modernization at all costs. The dams would be built, reining in a fickle river, the countryside electrified, the yokels put to work, their children educated and enriched. Out of this literal backwater would come streaming the currents of progress.

The TVA now operates forty-nine dams along the Tennessee River's many branches. In the fifties and onwards, the TVA began expanding its energy portfolio by constructing coal, gas, and nuclear power plants next to reservoirs on the Tennessee. Today, the TVA's properties encompass 293,000 acres of riverside and 650,000 acres of surface water. From all this acreage—gifted to the TVA by the federal government—the Authority generates 158.4 billion kilowatts of electricity and $11.2 billion in revenue each year. (In fiscal year 2019, Jeff Lyash, the TVA's top executive, was compensated $8.3 million, making him the federal government's highest-paid employee.) Although the Authority's image is intentionally linked to hydropower ("The Original Green Power," declares the TVA's website), only eleven percent of its present output is generated by dams, while thirty-nine percent comes from nuclear, twenty-six percent from gas, nineteen percent from coal, and only four percent from wind and solar.

A few years ago, I started revisiting the Tennessee River and its tributaries every time I went home, trying to get a closer look at the TVA's dams. I drove up to Norris Dam, the TVA's first completed project, a magisterial concrete slab that impedes the Clinch River. I got out of my car and walked to the dam's top. Swallows feasted on flies above the spillway. A woman in a red Corvette parked her car in the middle of traffic and snapped a quick picture of Norris Lake.

I remember growing up in this valley and not even noticing the dams, which despite their unnatural appearance had always seemed to me like signs of safety, these giant walls protecting me as I swam. Back then, I didn't think about what was under the lakes or how radically a dam can change a river. The TVA relocated fifteen thousand families to make room for its reservoirs. Landowners were compensated for their farms, while sharecroppers and squatters received nothing. Some locals resisted, spurning both payouts and pressure from their neighbors in order to delay construction. When warned by TVA executives that her land would be flooded whether she stayed or not, a local woman living on what became Norris Lake reportedly responded, "Well, I'll stay here until the water comes up, and flow down with it when it does."

The TVA's story is far from exceptional. The United States has built approximately 84,000 dams—that's an average of one dam every day since the Declaration of Independence—and China has constructed a similar number since the 1960s. All over the world, nations are still damming rivers, often in rural regions populated by the Indigenous and the poor. I cannot claim to have a clear cost-benefit analysis for any of these projects—it seems impossible, after all, to weigh kilowatts against communities drowned—and in any case, a dam's upside for its builders is not just electricity, but a monumental sense of control.

Standing on Norris Dam in 2021, I remembered how the river that was really a creek had ended. The river ran through private property, and the farmer who owned that property eventually cut down all the trees, leaving behind a mess of felled limbs spanning the valley I'd once treated as my own. By that point, the river had already been declining for several years, slowing down into a muddy marsh, but the farmer's actions dealt the river a decisive blow. I equated my little river's end, in my journal, to the "desecration of my childhood," and for many weeks afterward, I kept returning to the river's remains, embroiled in this feeling I now recognize as grief.

V. REMEMBRANCE

In 1988, the French immunologist Jacques Benveniste published a paper in *Nature* about "water memory." Benveniste's team diluted antibody-rich solutions until they were effectively pure water. Miraculously, this water, when introduced to human basophil cells, still triggered an immune response. The study concluded that water molecules can sometimes lock into patterns surrounding a foreign agent, so that even when that agent disappears, the water retains the shape of its presence. If this was true, then water was a text filled with meaningful gaps, a codex of absences the human immune system might homeopathically respond to, mistaking bullet holes for bullets.

When I was sixteen, one of the largest riparian disasters in American history occurred in the Tennessee River Valley. A TVA coal plant had been storing fly ash in an unlined retention pond near where the Clinch and Emory Rivers converged. A few days before Christmas 2008, the walls of the pond failed, injecting the river with a billion gallons of arsenic and selenium-laced ash. Gray sludge engulfed three hundred acres of shoreline, including the tiny town of Swan Pond. In some areas, the layer of toxic grime was over six feet deep and littered with recently asphyxiated fish.

I heard a lot about the spill from teachers at school, but it was actually quite easy to ignore that I, too, shared a watershed with the people and animals who'd borne the brunt of the damage—that the Tennessee ran through all of us, from water tap to sewer. I lived only a dozen miles upstream from the spill site, and for the rest of high school, I kept going down to the river with my friends, kept joking there was "something in the water," but always with the supposition that that "something" could never hurt us.

TVA hired Jacobs Solutions, a Texas-based conglomerate, to clean up its mess, and Jacobs Solutions contracted nine hundred men in the greater Knoxville area to work seven days a week at the spill site, often without proper protective gear or hazardous-materials training. In the years since, thirty-six of those workers have died and hundreds of others have developed respiratory problems, chest pain, impotency, and various cancers of the blood, skin, and lungs—all indications of heavy metal poisoning. Both Jacobs Solutions and the TVA have denied all liability for the workers' ailments. Litigation is pending, and likely will remain so until all the workers have settled, or succumbed. A TVA spokeswoman interviewed for a *60 Minutes* segment on the spill described fly ash as essentially benign. She told Lesley Stahl that she'd even be willing to swim in the contaminated part of the river, though an exhibition dip was never arranged.

Benveniste's results were never corroborated in independent labs. As far as science is concerned, the theory of water memory has been soundly debunked. Still, it seems undeniable that bodies of water recall, as humans do, the flickers of past events. When Jacobs Solutions' contractors were dredging ash up from the riverbed, they also brought up sediment containing cesium-137, a radioactive isotope associated with nuclear disasters. Cesium-137 is not a known component of fly ash, but it is produced as a byproduct of nuclear fission. A stop-work order was issued. The men got out of the water.

Here is where the river's biography gets even more complicated. Not far upstream from the spill site lies Oak Ridge National Lab, a once-secret production site for weapons-grade uranium. During World War II, scientists at Oak Ridge took raw uranium sourced from mines in colonial Congo and enriched it. They did this via processes partly powered by TVA dams, helping produce the atomic bombs the US later dropped on Japan. To this day, twelve million cubic yards of radioactive waste remains unaccounted for on the Oak Ridge Reservation. Where all these byproducts went—where they continue to go, radiant, refulgent—has long been a subject of local rumor. As for the supposedly harmless ash dredged up from the river, the TVA had it carried hundreds of miles away to a landfill in the Alabama Black Belt—a nonproblem for another town, another river.

It's tempting to take a hardline position against developing any river, to blame all a river's problems on the Manhattan Project, the TVA, or some other enterprise of government or war. The illogic of such a position is twofold. First, it dismisses out of hand the opinions of local people who are quick to sing a dam's praises and who believe, wholeheartedly, that human control over a river has helped better their livelihoods. Second, it imputes an Edenic past to the river, a past the river would revert to if only the dams could be dismantled and all the trace metals magicked away. So often what damming supplants, though, is not a primeval, innocent river—an ecological childhood—but a waterscape already defined by its past. A river's memory is reliably long.

Prior to their removal in the 1830s, during which the US government used the river to transport thousands of Cherokees west, dispossessing them of their natal lands and waters, the Cherokee people and their ancestors made their homes in the upper Tennessee Valley. Rivers and streams played—and continue to play—a central role in Cherokee culture and social life. To the Cherokee, the Tennessee is Gunahita Asgaya, or "Long Man," a body of water with its head in the mountains and its feet in the valley. Cherokees named not just sections of the river but specific points along its length, providing anchors for cultural memory. Their oral stories—the oldest of which are called "wonder stories" by ethnographers—make frequent reference to where along the river a story takes place, suturing fantastical happenings and interdimensional portals to physical, lived-in sites. When articulating interclan relations, Cherokees spoke of being *tsa'gi*, upstream, or *ge'i*, downstream, from different kin. The river land's first residents did not consider the river as fully separable from themselves or seek total dominion over its course. This does not mean they did not change the river, existing naively in its presence (see the prevalent trope of the "ecological Indian"). According to the Cherokee Riverkeepers website, Cherokees actively modified and maintained the riverine landscape. They widened its banksides for agriculture, erected stone weirs in the current to catch fish, and built populous settlements along the river's length. Today, the Eastern Band of Cherokee—the descendants of those who evaded removal—still live by the Oconaluftee, a tributary of the Tennessee, and regularly monitor the river's health.

I do not know what it is to hold such long-standing ties to a river, though I think I have experienced, with my own little river, the severing of a water-based bond. I want to learn how to form ties to new waterways while also honoring riparian pasts; how to connect to land and waterscapes in a longitudinal, accumulative way—the way of constant return, but not always to one's origins.

VI. COMPARISON

The poet Du Fu once lived by a tributary of the Minjiang River, itself a tributary of the Yangtze. He kept a thatch hut by the water that's been turned into a museum today. After many years of vagrancy, Du Fu's riverside hut on the outskirts of Chengdu provided a semblance of calm: *We linger out flawless, dusk-tinted / blossoms on water—a world enough / now, / enough and more.* Even in that peaceful place, the poet could not suppress his restless nature. He turned his back on Chengdu, traveling by boat to the Yangtze's Three Gorges. There he settled in the village of Kuizhou, at the southern limit of what was then considered the Chinese realm. *Ten years / A guest of lakes and rivers,* he wrote. *My heart of lingering dusk grows / boundless.*

During my time in Chengdu, I also once ventured into the Gorges. I arrived in Yichang, at the Gorges' easternmost point, and walked down to the concrete-lined river. Directly upstream from Yichang is the world's largest dam, Three Gorges Dam, a project that took nearly twenty years and the relocation of thirteen major cities to complete. Like the TVA dams, the Three Gorges project supports a narrative of modernization, but also national pride. Sun Yat-sen alluded to the dam's possibility in his "Three Principles of the People," Chiang Kai-shek sent surveyors into the Gorges to scope out possible sites, and Chairman Mao himself prophesied the dam's completion in a poem, writing that "across the western Jiang we shall erect a wall of stone."

I went to see that wall where it bisected the river. I stood at a lookout above the dam, rain lashing my umbrella, trying to take in the magnitude of what I saw: that godlike countenance, that stoppered valley. There was no possible vantage from which I could see all of it. Gray concrete studded with red towers; power lines cutting the humid and heavy air; islands in the reservoir that used to be hilltops.

In an article on Three Gorges Dam, Peter Hessler, *The New Yorker*'s longtime China correspondent, compared the Yangtze Valley to the "middle of Appalachia." Both regions have long been considered unproductive, expendable: places easily sacrificed to a river. The same triumphal narrative I'd once believed about the TVA could now be retold on a grander scale. The dams would be built, reining in a mighty river; the countryside electrified, the yokels put to work, their children educated and enriched. Out of this literal backwater would come streaming the currents of progress.

As the dam neared completion, local officials marked the Gorges' sides with long black lines indicating where the water level would rise. Anything sitting below these lines would have to be moved or abandoned. What became of the rice fields, the livestock and pets? What happened to the undiscovered relics in the caves, the tiny outpost where Du Fu wrote so many of his poems, the 1.5 million people who had to move away? Much of it is underwater now, I assume. A dam is skilled at covering its tracks.

VII. FORGETTING

My home state and its river both take their names from Tanasi, one of several "Overhill" Cherokee towns that once thrived by the Little Tennessee. Although many Cherokee still live within the Tennessee River watershed, the town of Tanasi, or what remained of it, has for decades been underwater. In 1979, the TVA completed Tellico Dam, and the river, rising up in its basin, reclaimed its own name.

After driving away from Norris Dam, I followed the river system south, stopping at the Tanasi Memorial on my way over to Watts Barr Dam. The TVA has set up a little park near Vonore commemorating Tanasi and some of the other Cherokee towns now consumed by the dam's reservoir. The official memorial sits just a few feet shy of the river, a grim pentagon of stone. I read the text on the plaque: TANASI CAPITAL OF THE CHEROKEE NATION ... LOCATED 300 YARDS WEST OF THIS MARKER. A little way down the shore, I also read a posted notice reminding me that "removal of artifacts or destruction of sites is punishable by law." The notice ended with an exhortation to "help protect the past for future generations," the past being three hundred yards away and impounded by a river.

VIII. RELINQUISHMENT

If you divide the length of a river's banks by that of a straight line drawn from its headwaters to its mouth, you can obtain a measure of the river's windiness—what hydrologists call "sinuosity," but which I like to think of as a river's penchant for diversion. A mathematician once hypothesized that the average sinuosity of all Earth's rivers must be 3.14, or pi. This mathematician proposed that each of a river's many curves could be thought of as the aqueous arcs of a circle. Summing the lengths of a river's meanders gives the circle's circumference, and drawing a straight line from the river's headwaters to its mouth gives the circle's diameter. Solving for sinuosity would result, if you recall middle-school geometry, in pi. No one has calculated the average sinuosity of all Earth's rivers yet, though someone did try in 2015. After 254 rivers, the number they had was 1.94, not pi.

More than two thousand years ago, the governor of Sichuan, a man named Li Bing, also tried rationalizing a river. Rather than build a permanent dam, Bing's engineers created an island of sand and stone and inserted it into the middle of the Minjiang, dividing the river into two separate streams at a spot called Dujiangyan. One of these streams was then diverted into a network of irrigation canals that still serves the Chengdu Plain today. Historians often cite Dujiangyan as an ancient example of Chinese engineering's concordance with nature: instead of simply blocking the river, Li Bing's engineers worked in tandem with its flow properties and topography to achieve similar ends. During the winter, when water levels are low, temporary dams were still placed in the river, birthing a local tradition. The governor of Sichuan would travel from Chengdu to Dujiangyan each spring to give offerings at a temple dedicated to Li Bing before presiding over a ceremonial breaking of dams. The Minjiang would gush forth in a great welter, and the governor, borne aloft by his chair bearers, would set off at a fast clip for Chengdu, trying to beat the water.

Dams are still being built, turning rivers into dead water, but dams are also being removed, or left unrealized in their blueprint phase. In 2012 and 2014, after years of activism led by the Lower Elwha Klallam Tribe in collaboration with biologists and environmental advocates, two aging dams on Washington's Elwha River were breached, restoring the river's age-old salmon runs. (A similar, even larger undamming project is now underway on the Klamath River.) China is still pouring money into hydroelectric development, both within its own borders and throughout the Global South, but local dissent has managed, for now, to forestall a plan for thirteen dams on the Nujiang River, in the Three Parallel Rivers region of China. The Nujiang is China's last undammed river; it both nourishes and carves a valley rich in endemic animals and plants. I took a trip there with my partner during my last stint in China. We did not swim in the river, whose current can be deadly, but we hiked up high to see the river from above, and felt its call in our bloodstreams as we danced at night in a village overlooking the Nujiang's first, tea-colored bend.

A river cannot be told by its numbers; it is a circle that does not close. The unclosed circle says that what has been lost cannot be recovered, that life is time flowing past and sweeping us away. What a river also is, according to my mother, is desire: a force propelling us toward the other. She did not say this to me in so many words. What she said was a Chinese idiom: 船到桥头自然直. I was about to leave for China yet again when she said this to me, heartsick on account of a man—the same man I would later take to the river. Having forgotten all the idioms I learned in Chinese school, I asked my mother to please explain. She told me that when a boat on a river comes to a bridge, it can only commit to the river. The boat is you, she said. The river is how you feel, and when the boat is carried by the river to a crucial point, your feelings will narrow, offering no choice but forward. I thought about the problem man as if he were a bridge. I thought of myself as a boat on a river, slipping under and through him. I felt better.

Du Fu never dreamt of defying his river. When the waters came up, he flowed down with them, dying aboard a boat that foundered on the Yangtze's current. Maybe this is the river's only instruction, the one most difficult to follow: Don't turn away, don't balk. What happens next is up to the water.

IX. RELATION

In 2017, a river in New Zealand achieved, by writ of law, the same rights and protections as a person. Settlers call the river Whanganui. It is known to the local Māori *iwi* (tribe) as Te Awa Tupua. The agreement reached between the Whanganui iwi and the New Zealand government defines the river as such:

(a) the body of water known as the Whanganui River that flows continuously or intermittently from its headwaters to the mouth of the Whanganui River on the Tasman Sea and is located within the Whanganui River catchment; and

(b) all tributaries, streams, and other natural watercourses that flow continuously or intermittently into the body of water described in paragraph (a) and are located within the Whanganui River catchment; and

(c) all lakes and wetlands connected continuously or intermittently with the bodies of water referred to in paragraphs (a) and (b) and all tributaries, streams, and other natural watercourses flowing into those lakes and wetlands; and

(d) the beds of the bodies of water described in paragraphs (a) to (c).

Relation emerges from totality: a river of interrelated, inextricable parts. The people of Whanganui's iwi are also in relation to the river, as the river's legal representatives but also its residents, its kinfolk, its keepers. "*Ko au te awa. Ko te awa ko au*," Whanganui's relatives have long said. "I am the river. The river is me."

There is an important difference between turning a river into a personal metaphor for life—claiming it as yours—and treating the river as its own, system-creating entity. The search for a river's origin ignores all but the main channel; it does not see the river as an "indivisible and living whole . . . incorporating all its physical and metaphysical elements," a whole that does not begin anywhere, but rather sets out from many places at once. To imagine the river as one line and to go looking for its headwaters is to seek selfhood in the singular. Even my little river, the one I littered with names, was never so simple, rising instead from countless seeps and percolations in the surrounding hills. It is from so many scattered points that a river gathers its materials.

Lives, too, are overdetermined, derived from every possible source. While the Yangtze and the Oujiang never meet (except in their mutual sink, the Pacific), in my family, they form a shared watershed with the Tennessee. Three rivers: two facing east and one facing west, our waters all mixing in the middle. I've gone prospecting up this braided channel, seeking vicarious memories and the fountain-like spring that river people like me are fond of imagining. I've stood by what I am told are the rivers of my parents and their parents, water running away at my feet, and traced what it is that connects me to these places and these places to me—the answer, of course, being a river.

I hear the river is / broken / Wide open, writes Du Fu, *gathering every / distance into one.*

X.CONTINUANCE

I drove down the Tennessee's valley, making pit stops at every dam: Watts Bar, Chickamauga, Nickajack, Guntersville, Wheeler, and Wilson. I stopped for the night in the city of Muscle Shoals, Alabama. Before the TVA built all of its dams, the Shoals were the Tennessee's shallowest, most treacherous miles. There's an old Indian mound across the water in Florence that dates to the Woodland period. I drove over there and took the stairs to its top. That night, I would pay much more than expected for a room in a hotel above a bowling alley.

I would stay up, sleepless, listening to the balls as they rolled, the pins falling before them. I would walk downtown to order polenta and two Old-Fashioneds at a French restaurant next to a Billy Reid boutique. I would forget to feed the meter.

Betwixt and before all this, I say hello to the river. A few canoers are out there, their fishing lines baited and cast. Although I never located its source, I know the nameless river once emptied into a branch of the Little Turkey Creek, which in turn empties into the Tennessee, which many miles and dams later passes by the Shoals, and from here on continues, as rivers do, meeting the Ohio near Paducah and the Mississippi near Cairo, the river that finally brings this water down to the sea. Those now-deceased waters, the ones I remember so well, they'd been headed to this place before I even knew it existed. How exhausting it can be, the river's continuity; how bolstering, too, that through all befores and afters, a river still bends.

Queer Cartographies

One of the first stories I read on queeringthemap.com (QTM) goes like this: "故事从这里开始," says a bubble of text, or "The story starts from here."

The story happened on the outskirts of a midsize Chinese city. Like most of the other posts embedded in QTM, its author and date are unknown. I sit in my Cambridge apartment, the one I share with my partner, envisaging a pair of baby dykes in tracksuit school uniforms, trading glances from across a crowded street. Maybe the two not-yet-girlfriends are standing right where the map says they are—at the terminus of an alleyway in Nanchang, Jiangxi Province. Sunlight bears down on them from above. A trash picker coasts by on his bike. One of the girls wants more than anything to wave at the other girl, but she doesn't, and in later years, she will think that this is how they began, as a missed connection singed on both ends.

The scene shifts, taking the story elsewhere. In the capital, they wax poetic—

The secrets of sweetness and bravery are hidden in those words, printed on the asphalt floor of the alley that we traveled day and night. They are water steam that floats gently in the air of that courtyard. The leaves, the walls, the windows, they know everything. (Beijing)

and in the largest city, they write smut—

At the hotel room you laughed and said I was "so fat" in the most bluntly Chinese way possible after I took my clothes off, but we still had great sex and I spent at least an hour rimming that sweet, sweet hole (my first time giving a rimjob—thank you for helping me realise that I love to eat ass!). (Shanghai)

After the tryst, the queer ranges, footloose and anxious, down the Pacific coast—

I am asexual. I didn't know. (Zhuhai)

they slip over the border at Lo Wu—

stayed here with you at your grandma's 嫲嫲 place and she will probably never know all the shameful things you wanted to do to me. (Hong Kong)

to catch their flight across the straits:

Where you danced to 40 something of my parents friends because you loved me. I will remember it always and forever and love you endlessly for. 33 years of knowing a city and you made me love it so much more in a few short days. I love you pretty girl. 最佳女友. (Taipei)

These are the kinds of moments plotted into QTM, an online "counter-mapping platform" that records the "cartography of queer life." Visually, QTM resembles Google Maps, only overlaid by a pink filter and deprived of its navigational search bar. The map's major roads are yellow, its bodies of water periwinkle. When a user logs a queer moment onto QTM, it shows up like a pushpin on a corkboard, a pin affixed to a note. These notes are all over the place, geographically, emotionally. Some are acts of desultory documentation: "@toddjhammond - Proposed to my Husband 07 January, 2017" (Hilo). Others dabble in fan fiction—"I was in that nightclub in R'lyeh, I saw your tentacles, and I instantly loved you" (somewhere in the South Pacific)—or cover song—"I felt you in my legs, before I ever met you" (Montreal)—or amateur erotica, the very best kind—"When the preacher fucked me he said 'You are mine, you are mine' " (Juazeiro).

Many moments shoot for the poignant and get there, the map a repository for the shipwrecked remnants of transatlantic love affairs, the late-coming assertions of self-ownership and self-worth, the gender apologia, the private memorials to getting laid or coming out: "Stood here and screamed 'I'm a lesbian' into the tree line. Even at that volume I couldn't convince myself. But the word queer has stuck hard and fast. I'm grateful to the trees for holding me in that moment" (Providence).

QTM itself began with a tree: a silver maple in Montreal's Jeanne-Mance Park. Lucas LaRochelle, QTM's designer, was biking past this tree when the idea for an online queer map first came to them. LaRochelle had met a former partner at the tree's base, someone who'd eventually reset the entire landscape of what being queer meant to them. "I felt connected not only to that partner or that tree," LaRochelle said in an interview, "but to the feeling of queerness that seemed to have lingered at that spot despite the passage of time."

ROOM

I met my first boyfriend in a tiny college town not far from the Mississippi. We were both attending a summer camp called Governor's School, where ambitious high schoolers from Tennessee went through the motions of collegiate life.

Let's call the boy John. He was a rower from Chattanooga, tall and athletic with a slightly disorganized face. I first saw John at a laundry room "rave" organized by one of my friends. MGMT's "Just Kids" was playing, a Party City light weakly strobing in one corner. I watched John dancing by the driers with a crown of Dollar Tree glow sticks on his head and wanted him exactly like that: sweaty tank top and sunburned arms, neon freckles on his face.

The boys' dorm was full of rooms left unoccupied for the summer. Each looked identical to all the others, with a single slit window, a pair of wooden desks, spring-loaded mattresses, and a mirror on one wall. I remember the room's number, 109; I remember when John entered, shutting the door behind him, how the air inside 109 shifted to accommodate a new presence. From then on, it was like that summer had a front office, which we were a part of, taking classes and talking shit, but there was also this backroom reserved just for us, a space we returned to

whenever we could. We stayed up together in that room, practicing acts of clumsy largesse on each other. He liked picking
me up and placing me on the desk, my bare ass against the wall
as he fellated. I liked unfurling against the raft of his height, a
canvas stretching taut on its frame.

That we'd soon walk out of that room and, after a few
months' time, out of each other's lives was already a given. The
room would remain exactly as we'd found it: a passive recepta-
cle for temporary tenants. Before we left, we strip-mined those
walls of every feeling that we could; we examined each other's
inches, we talked about what we saw. On the last night of camp,
just hours before our parents came to pick us up, I remember
John and I standing together in the middle of the room, naked,
watching the two boys taking shape in the mirror, the taller
one's arms wrapped around the shorter one's waist, their every
extremity erect. Our two bodies in the mirror were like a proof
of concept. The chamber was now active. My task was to continually reconstitute this space.

If every map is essentially a claim that whatever it shows exists,
then a map chock-full of queer moments asserts that queerness—
the lived experiences of gay and lesbian people, bi people, intersex,
trans, and other gender-nonconforming people, ace people, two-
spirit people, gradients and hairsplittings of all of the above—
exists, not just abstractly, but as identities and bodies attached to
specific points in space. That QTM makes this assertion over and
over again is important, because the world at present is still a heteronormative one in which straightness prevails as a kind of moral
standard and sexual default.

To be clear, heteronormativity is not what some straight allies seem to think it is: an anachronistic, prudish mindset held only by religious conservatives and bigots. In an essay called "Sex in Public," the queer theorists Lauren Berlant and Michael Warner define heteronormativity as "this sense of rightness—embedded in things and not just in sex." Heteronormativity acts on us regardless of our politics or our pronouns, convincing us that there is a "normal" way of loving and fucking, laboring and budgeting, child-rearing and taking out the trash. The point here is not to thumb one's nose at the straights and their funny pastimes, especially when these pastimes are held sacred by many a queer; the point is to recognize a social script in action, and to consider what it might entail to start unlearning that script. "Heterosexuality involves so many practices that are not sex that a world in which this hegemonic cluster would not be dominant is, at this point, unimaginable," write Berlant and Warner. "We are trying to bring that world into being."

Perhaps LaRochelle's map is also trying to help queers visualize such an alternative world. Held under the most flattering of lights, QTM stages a queer takeover of the map, rehashing cartographically the old Queer Nation slogan of "We're here. We're queer. Get used to it." And yet, so many of the queer moments that appear on this map are momentary, ephemeral—not exactly the building blocks of a distinctive gay cosmos. Queer institutions are obviously present, semipermanent structures that queers have made and maintained for years, from health clinics to archives, but QTM offers little guidance on how to find such spaces. Instead, what the map collects are all those curious loci that have proved integral to the shaping of individual queer lives: highly personal points of reference, now shared to QTM.

I started spending a lot more time consulting the map in 2020, just as COVID-19 began to careen, a wrecking ball studded with spike proteins, through our collective lives, leaving a slew of shuttered spaces—queer ones, especially, it seemed—in its wake. Much of my life up to that point had felt like a prolonged process of coming out, not from the closet (that disclosure happened abruptly, and without much fanfare), but into a world full of gay bars and saunas, impromptu dance parties and all-queer writing retreats—places in which I could comfortably be queer. Now that "going out" had a different, potentially unethical meaning, I had to relearn how to be queer in an internalized, static way; to stay in with my desires, to sit with them for hours at a time.

This period of turning inward had actually preceded the pandemic. By 2020, I'd been in a committed relationship with another man for several years, and many of the activities I'd once associated with my queerness—watching artsy films, fucking, gossiping about friends—had already turned into activities I mostly enjoyed inside, with one person. My partner and I had lived in four cities together. Our lives had solidified into a categorically domestic arrangement. I couldn't sleep anymore without his back against mine in the bed, two little spoons touching. He put the coffee on and split all my bills. His workdays defined what hours I wrote and read. Early in the pandemic, we decided to share our locations with each other on our phones—a perhaps unnecessary gesture, since our geodata, in more ways than one, basically overlapped.

Even before the pandemic decisively sealed us in, I was already asking myself if this was it: my queer moments all concentrated in one person, one place. Though we still went out in those days, the gay clubs in Providence and Boston had all started to feel a bit pat. Now that I was barred from accessing even those spaces, unsure if they'd be open when next we came out, I found myself turning to QTM's entries as a kind of substitute for lost space. The stories on the map supplemented my other reading, which, since I was studying for my PhD qualifying exams that year, included a lot of books on queer theory. One could spend forever reading in this vein, conceptualizing and reassessing what it means to be queer, but it's something else entirely to watch actual queer people put themselves on a map. Looking at QTM, I met so many people I can't ever know who were still *my people*. So many voices speaking in other rooms, echolocating, seeing in their minds the contours of a queerness they swore had been *here*, pinned to this very spot.

TRACK

"Hey girls, it's time to go back!" yelled Coach Crawford. "Oh, and you too, Thomas."

All the other boys were down at the end of the track, snickering at the coach's comic timing (gender, the oldest of jokes). I was one of the girls, or I was boyhood inflected by girldom: swishy, impure, a sliver of flesh at which the real boys liked to throw rocks.

Coach Crawford was supposed to be teaching us about "wellness," which at my high school meant abstinence propaganda and Maslow's hierarchy of needs. Every other lesson was spent walking down on the track. I walked beside two girls, Ellen and Erin, two girls who didn't always feel like girls to themselves. They'd deduced my queerness early on in the year, summoning it out of my mouth over the foursquare court (it shocked me when, after a beat, our game simply went on). We called ourselves "The Cock Connoisseurs," although the only cock any of us had ever seen was my own, scientifically examined one night at Ellen's house after we got into her mother's wine. Covetous by nature, we kept a roster of all the boys whose cocks we thought worthy of us—the green-eyed skater kid, the actor's broody son, the Mormon pole vaulter with the impressively honed traps. We Sharpied their names onto the wall in one of the gym's stairwells and weighed their attributes while walking endlessly around the track, often straying into that uneven margin where upkeep gave way to decadence. We were ribald, and we were raw, sleazy and silly and proud of our own ostentation. We walked—or rather, we circled—around and around the track's outermost circumference, playing Do, Die, or Marry with all the boys we'd trapped in our enclosure.

Over the last few months, I've been asking my queer friends to tell me about their own queer cartographies. My friend Ally, the one other practicing homosexual in my PhD cohort, tells me that being queer, for her, has always felt like more of an "orientation" than an "identity"—a feeling tantamount to gravity that drew her into the orbit of other queer women, while also inclining her toward certain political commitments and cultural fascinations (WNBA games and Cheryl Dunye's *The Watermelon Woman*). Talking to Ally reminds me of Sara Ahmed's book *Queer Phenomenology* (incidentally, one of LaRochelle's favorite queer theory texts), in which queerness gets redefined as "a matter of residence; of how we inhabit spaces as well as 'who' or 'what' we inhabit spaces with." This is not to say that queerness is environmentally determined as opposed to innate. Ahmed's point is much more fecund than the nurture-versus-nature debates that have so often gripped popular narratives about queer people and why we exist. Whether one believes their queerness stems from a chromosomal tea dance inside, neurodiversity or social awkwardness, a ring of keys jangling in a UPS Store outside of Cincinnati, or a calico dress they put on once in their grandmother's Daytona boudoir, being queer is first and foremost what one does with their queer desires, the "lifelines" they build out from every closet, lines which for many queers often run perpendicular to those inherited from the straights.

According to Ahmed, a queer life is one that proceeds down certain pathways and not others, a life spent steadfastly facing the wrong direction, eyes leveled on the "opposite gender" bathroom, the darkened nook at the back of the bar. These chosen misalignments—when a queer is "walking astray"—can feel comforting, like sliding one's feet into a worn-in pair of Birkenstocks, or epochal, like introducing a new partner to one's homophobic parents. Either way, these motions take conviction to make and then repeat, for heteronormativity doesn't only point us toward prescribed objects of desire like family life, mortgages, purity myths, and earning beaucoup bucks, it goads us down those pathways by proffering spiritual and monetary carrots, and by bringing the hammer down when needed. In order for queerness to exist, we require much more than just the wiliness to evade the heterosexual bait and switch. We need somewhere to go: a destination, however dubious, to seek.

Wherever that idealized queer space might be, most queers devote a lot of time and energy to searching for it. To make a map of such itineraries is a strange endeavor, like trying to photograph the wind. Putting queer lives in spatial terms gives to the Q-word a context, and like some kind of chameleonic ectoplasm, our queer experiences morph in response to their environs. In Seoul, it is the "elevator cctv of our last kiss sleepy fluorescent a little cold, but warm all the same." In Udine, it's "coke for you," which may be a soft drink, an allusion to the Frank O'Hara poem, or drugs. In Ulaanbaatar, it's "July 2008, in the airport at 3am. I realised I didn't just want to be a man—I was already one." QTM provides not a faithful depiction of the world as it is or was or even will be, but a locational service for navigating territories of fleeting experience, worlds built not to last, but to deviate and diverge.

On QTM, queer moments crop up almost everywhere, though certain epicenters carry more of the load than others. Berlin, London, Paris, and San Francisco. Palm Springs and Key West. Oberlin, Tufts, and any of the Seven Sisters. New York, always New York.

While studying biology in college, I somehow maneuvered my way into a summer internship at a luxury fashion retailer based in one of queer life's most storied spaces. My internship had nothing to do with being queer, but my cubicle was in a bustling glass tower, and that glass tower was in New York. At the company where I worked, employees appointed themselves in Proenza dresses and Jil Sander knits. I felt glamorous even fetching Starbucks for them or returning their unwanted Tibi shoes to Saks.

The anthropologist Kath Weston writes of a "sexual geography in which the city represents a beacon of tolerance and gay community, the country a locus of persecution and gay absence." According to Weston, coming out of the closet for queers is synonymous with *coming in* to the city. This "Great Gay Migration" is driven by a multitude of factors, but especially by the idea that cities provide queers both relief from homophobic harassment and the freedom to act and associate as they choose. My own tropism toward urban life probably began with the e-catalog at my hometown library. It was there that I first encountered the writings of gay male authors like Alan

Hollinghurst, Andrew Holleran, Edmund White, and Jim Grimsley, all of whom had written stories set in some version of "the City." In short, the City was where one went to find a livable gay life. The City was fashion and music and smoking on a stoop after priapic rounds of sex. The City was a generator of untold possibilities, of late afternoons spent cruising in bulrushy parks and sunrises glimpsed while heading home from the baths.

What I failed to register about this City was that it no longer existed, at least not in the iteration I'd read so much about—the free-wheeling, hedonic gay world of New York, San Francisco, and London in their pre-Reagan, pre-Thatcher, pre-AIDS salad days. At twenty, I walked around Manhattan for hours, looking for that lost city, lust-ing not after specific men but the unspecifiable dream of yesterday's queer urbanism, this eros made public, this dancer inseparable from the dance. I'd leave my office after work each day and walk south down Broadway to Soho, where dinner would happen, if it happened at all, upright outside Dean & DeLuca. I'd walk through Chinatown and the Bowery, Little Italy, FiDi, the slanting rays of Greenwich Village, killing time until I could try my luck at Splash! in Chelsea—a gay nightclub where the bouncer sometimes didn't mind my brother's expired ID—and afterward, I'd wind up somewhere near the Hud-son, in the Meatpacking District, for instance, where there were Korean art students going hard against the cobblestones in new-season Nicholas Kirkwoods, and lights still on in the Marni store at One Gansevoort, and out-of-towners like me with haircuts I'd call "current" standing rank and file outside the Standard Hotel, looking bored but feeling, I'm sure of it, just as excited as I was to be there in that sopping New York June.

In all those hours of aimless ambulation, I never met anyone, never got up the nerve to take or be taken. I think I was rather lonely that summer in the City, but I was also too unused to the feeling, its cool creep across my skin, to ever name it as such. I confused my loneliness with longing, my singleness with freedom. I saw myself as a queer person seeking his own private corner of the world, somewhere set aside and governed by different rules. Wasn't being queer a denial of the usual attachments, the daily cling wrap of work meetings and text threads with Mom? Wasn't aloneness its own queer rite of passage, this room where one could finally live by and for themself?

I knew that room much better than the city that contained it—the sublet in West Harlem I retreated to every night. That room was in a two-bed, one-bath apartment I split with a jazz pianist, her brindled cat, and a tutor dealing in SATs. It had a bed and a stool and a clothes rack in one corner. It had two curtainless windows looking out on a narrow breezeway, and beyond that, an impassive wall of brick. This room reminded me of all the rooms in the gay novels I'd read, rooms where queers went to stew in their own, often self-destructive tendencies. For the narrator of Edmund White's *The Beautiful Room Is Empty*, this room's location doesn't really matter. It could be a drafty garret in Ann Arbor or a borrowed condo in Chicago, as long as the space was tectonically unstable—a place to write and rut, but never to stay.

In his novel *Giovanni's Room*, James Baldwin describes the room in Paris shared by two lovers as "every room I had ever been in and every room I find myself hereafter," a space "not large enough for two." But oh, what a room it sometimes could be! What a delicate, clandestine scene! When I was younger and still new to every city, I very much wanted to be consumed by a room like that, to be at the center of a star as it collapsed. Equally, I wanted to flee as quickly as I could from any lightly furnished disaster, and these contradictory impulses—the one that drew me outward into the streets, and the other one that consigned me to a room's infinite involutions—came to define, for me, the disorienting geographies of being queer in my twenties.

CLUB

It's always the same story told by a different black box, and every gay man I know has complaints to air about it. "A sweltering, queeny meat rack," one friend calls it. A great place to go if you enjoy "feeling inadequate in every way," quips another. We gripe about the prices, the DJ, the overtures unreturned or unwanted. But each time we leave, it's with the knowledge we'll be back again. Our complaints are those of the already converted, the ones who keep willfully forgetting they've been here before, because hey, this time might be different.

I'm twenty and have one calf hooked around a pole in a renovated World War Two–era bunker in Shanghai. I'm twenty-six and waiting in line to pee at Petticoat Lane in Hong Kong. I'm twenty-six again in Berlin, outside on the rooftop, looking up at the TV Tower and babbling to a boy from Dubai about Isherwood and Auden. I'm twenty-two on the dance floor at TerMIX in Prague. I'm on the cusp of twenty-four at the EndUp in San Francisco, the back end of twenty-five at Blake's in Atlanta. I'm at Toilet Club and Akbar and Machine. I'm at Industry. I'm at Destination. I'm at Mixed Nuts and Nellie's and Underground and Moeem. I'm at Tribe before Play, Scarlet in Honolulu followed by Scarlet in Chicago. I'm at Club Café in Boston. Cover is ten and close is at two.

I'm seventeen, and it's finally the first time. The club is called the Carousel. Inside, Ellen, Erin, and I will dance in a sunken pit ringed by watchful men, all three of us chanting the lyrics to a song by Juvenile. We will charm a sickly-sweet drink from one of these men, and then we will go upstairs and watch the drag queens perform, their padded hips and painted faces showing us how. Before any of this can begin, though, I must hand my ID to the butch at the lectern with the binder full of underage faces. They put a bracelet on my wrist, gently, as one might apply a Band-Aid, and then nudge me toward the first of many doors.

Early in 2021, I taught a course at my university called "Mapping Desire: Queer Spaces in Contemporary Literature." We read Alison Bechdel and Carmen Maria Machado, Tommy Pico and Bryan Washington. I had my students write essays about the queer spaces they'd found on Tumblr and TikTok, at New England prep schools and socially distanced hyperpop concerts. Meanwhile, I played the part of the hipster nostalgist, harping on about how depressing it was to be discussing queer spaces in a time when we couldn't even physically share space with each other (the course met entirely on Zoom).

Each week, I found myself repeating the same basic lesson plan, encouraging my students to take a critical perspective on any representation of queer space, to question the vaunted benefits of gay and lesbian urbanism (What about gentrification and urban renewal? What about police brutality and the weaponizable rhetoric of safe spaces?), to problematize masculinist, colonial visions of virgin wilds and Mother Nature, to never stop asking the question: *Where do we go from here?* I wanted my students to experience queer space as I had learned to think of it: as an uncertainty principle. My trusty takeaway for each reading was this: There are no perfect queer spaces. There are only these experiments in what being queer can be, in this place, among these people, with this soundtrack and this quality of light.

Maybe it's the recurrent choosing of unideal places, then, that most defines a queer's relationship to space. My friend Bryant reflects that he's never found any queer space that didn't leave him feeling somewhat unfulfilled, and maybe that's what happens when the expectations are so high and the options so limited. Queer spaces do not so much liberate us from heteronormativity as press our faces against the smudged glass of an impossible freedom.

QTM also represents a queer world that is imperfect, provisional, at times even unsafe. Yes, this map can serve as a megaphone for expressing pride, both pride in oneself—"I exist, both lesbian and muslim and I'm not afraid anymore" (Mogadishu)—and one's place—"Rainbow Pride to remind us that Bangladesh has a history of queerness that is our own, not one co-opted by Western neoliberalism and the Pink Pound" (Dhaka). Yes, this map is a minefield of meaningful revelations: the "first strap-on" (Rome), the first "drunk buttfuck" (Corfu), the first time "I came out to you, one of my best friends from college, via Skype call" (Abuja). And yes, the entries on QTM are often records of resilience, homespun tales of queer people overcoming their odds: "This is a tiny Russian miner city near Vladivostok, where I met the love of my life. We are together for almost ten years. We have finished school together. Than—university. Than we have moved to Saint Petersburg. It is hard to be in homosexual relationships in Russia. But I regret nothing and I am a happy person" (Artyom).

But not every moment on QTM is one its cartographer would like to repeat. There are many pins that say, *Don't come here, beware—*

After talking about brotherhood between Jews and Muslims, we had sex in park next to the King David Hotel. As soon as he came, he tried to rob me. But it seemed so half-hearted that I knew he was just trying to save face. I took his hand off my collar and walked away. (Jerusalem)

Or even more searingly, this—

I was ashamed of who I was. The rolling hills that lived through thousands of blooming flowers. I saw a deer behind the pine. It was such a beautiful hike. I tried killing myself in the fields because of everything. It didn't work. (Laramie)

It didn't work. We broke up. They moved away. The life unlived goes on in perpetuity.

There is no way of apportioning where pride and privation should go on this map, no way of knowing with authority where a queer life will flourish and where it will wither on the vine. Several of my students made the point that it wasn't even just a case of straights storming queer spaces; that sometimes it was queer folks choosing to get in our own way. They described their own collegiate queer scene as a fortress maintained by vigilant gatekeeping, where almost everyone felt guilty of not being queer enough. Listening to them talk, I realized that one of the things I liked best about QTM is how thoroughly it pluralizes the idea of queer space, proving that queer moments happen anywhere and everywhere, not just in the erogenous zones dedicated to gay male nightlife, not just in coastal metropolises and the bubbles built by the liberal arts, not just on the street during the annual pride parade or on the silver screens and dog-eared pages of a horny and restive imagination. Queer spaces and all the many moments of confession, of hiding, of wound-licking and risk-taking they harbor are simultaneously multiplied and normalized by the map. They aren't sequestered from the public domain, and as a result, they lose some of their mystique, which isn't always a bad thing.

COMPASS

How does a queer find their way? I'm at the door of a bar named the Compass in Yunnan Province, watching a man watch me. I couldn't get back here if I tried, this sultry little dive by the Mekong that the local gays have claimed as their own. The man I came with is watching me leave with his friend, a look of gentlest rebuke on his face, as if to say, "Come and find me when you're done."

How does a queer find their way? Matthew tells me about his first summer of concatenating motion. He was eighteen and unwilling to wait, always riding the subway between the neighborhood in Brooklyn where his father was dying and those other neighborhoods in Manhattan where he went to fuck and introspect. "It was never any one space that did it for me," he says, but a "queer geometry of them."

How does a queer find their way? Cam grew into his queerness abroad, or rather in the constant shuttling between America and Asia. Queerness was culturally relative to him. It was the art of the code-switch, of being out in one country and closeted in another. A linguaphile by both nature and training, Cam learned that queerness, too, was a language, and that not all queer argots were the same. *Tongzhi. Okama. Gei.*

How does a queer find their way? Lauren was at a march protesting Trump when it hit her that hiding her bisexuality from her family was an obfuscation she could no longer afford. She'd already lived an optically straight, blond-haired and blue-eyed life in their eyes. Now was the time to name that other way.

Maybe we should be asking, instead: How can a queer get lost more often and more meaningfully? Not the vertices, but the lines, the vectors shooting outwards from each place. It's that look more than the bar that I remember, that look that fired like a bolt from inside the Compass's skittering dark; that look that pierced me, that seemed to know all the things in the world that I myself forgot.

A few years ago, I flew to Berlin to visit a museum full of queer memorabilia. The Schwules Museum ("Gay Museum" in English) is the oldest museum in the world dedicated to gay history. It was filled with posters from long-ago protests, DIY zines, and oil paintings that were vaguely pornographic. A photo slide machine ran on a loop in one corner, projecting onto the wall translucent images of queers and their chosen kin. I was there to research a paper on queer archives, but I was also thinking about the few, barely tangible objects that might comprise my own queer history museum: Grindr chat logs, a few tawdry nudes, receipts for well gin and tonics. "Nothing remains" would be the dramatic conclusion to reach here, though I think it's more accurate to say there was nothing I needed to keep.

I suppose this is why I far prefer reading the stories on QTM to adding my own. It's not that I think of my queer spaces as classified information—if that were the case, I would probably not include them in this essay—or that I literally don't know how to find them anymore on this map; it's that whatever made those spaces queer for me has usually gone away. And that feeling of intoxicated passion, of anarchic glee or restless becoming . . . it simply isn't there anymore. It's migrated to another site.

One of the queerest spaces I've ever experienced appeared for only a split second at the heart of a midsize Chinese city. I was out on a midnight run, and as I ran past the provincial government's imposing headquarters, I could see, through the barred metal fence posts and the lengthy shadows cast by a full moon, two uniformed guards sprinting full out by a reflecting pool on the fence's other side, two men laughing and shirking their duties for a breathless game of tag. I can supply no proof that these men felt anything but platonic affection for one another, but I know, as they know, that what went down by that reflecting pool was gay, gay, gay.

Thinking back to that moment, I realize my sense of its queerness depended at least partially on its backdrop: a brutalist government building in Changsha, not exactly a hotbed for queer release. The moment protruded for me. It stuck in my brain because such open homosocializing seemed, to quote Berlant and Warner, like "matter out of place." Any user of QTM will surely notice the relative density of queer moments in North America, Australia, New Zealand, and Western Europe compared to Africa, Asia, and the so-called "developing world." If queerness is not actually, as the Chinese politburo has recently been claiming, something imported from the West, then why are there so few queer moments in Cameroon and Nepal, Paraguay and Belarus? One obvious answer is that the map's users are mostly from the West and have charted their spaces accordingly. Another easy-to-reach conclusion is that the empty sectors on the map are more "traditional" or "homophobic" than the pin-filled bits. Queer people certainly live and love there, but they do so secretly, or under extreme duress. Some users of QTM have even chosen to speak on these silenced queers' behalf: "To any queer person out there: stay strong. Love will win eventually" (Windhoek); "You'll be okay. someone will accept you" (Sabha); "You are not alone! And love wins when we open up!" (Latakia).

I do not doubt that queers in many non-Western countries habitually experience violence and discrimination, nor would I rebuke any of these people for viewing the protections extended to gays in countries like mine as a glimmer of far-off hope. But the attainment of certain "gay rights" in the West should not so easily be conflated with a triumph for queers everywhere. Here in the US, where gay marriage is still legal for now and every straight person knows the name RuPaul, it may seem that our queer day in the sun has finally arrived, that this is the best it's likely to get, and that the kinds of queer spaces and structures we've created to house us are what gays the world over should strive for, should want. I'm not here to say that's wrong. I'm just here to say *not yet*.

BREEZEWAY

I used to rent an apartment in the desert with a courtyard and the filled-in outline of a pool. Whenever I felt lonely in that apartment, which was neither often nor rare, I went outside and sat in the breezeway just off the courtyard with my book. If a neighbor happened to walk past, I'd stub out my cigarette and playact like I was waiting on someone, a friend or lover, to arrive. The only thing I was waiting on was that time of day when the sun would gaze aslant through the stained-glass windows above the breezeway's entrance, cutting the beige hallway into diagonal bars of color. Mandarin orange and lime green.

As I write this, it's June 2021 in Chicago—Pride Month. I've come to Chicago to be the best man at my straight brother's wedding, and then to watch his cat while he honeymoons. My brother has lived in Boystown, America's oldest gayborhood, for most of the past decade. Before leaving on their trip, the newlyweds gift me one joint, two MDMA pills, and a note that reads, "Thank you, have fun."

Even with their blessing, I do not go out to the bars, all of which are open again. I spend my days like I used to, walking up and down the city's long vertebral column. Because it's Pride Month, there are rainbow dog bones being sold in Wrigleyville, rainbow flags anointing the Macy's downtown, rainbow mood lighting cast by the Ferris wheel at Navy Pier, an entire city aglow with bent and wonky light. Across the street from where my brother was wed, I see a billboard swarming with the names of different queer subreddits, from r/gaybros to r/NonBinary. Reddit's accompanying slogan: "Maybe you'll find yourself among people like you."

Did I mention that Lauren Berlant died this week, and I'm in my feelings about this and everything else? Berlant, who wrote in 1998 that the queer world they hoped to see was "a space of entrances, exits, unsystematized lines of acquaintance, projected horizons, typifying examples, alternate routes, blockages, incommensurate geographies." To be incommensurate is to be out of proportion, distended: a geography ill at ease with itself.

Just a few blocks west from where I'm writing this is Boystown's Legacy Walk, a series of rainbow-and-gold pylons honoring queer luminaries of the past. Each pylon looks kind of like a rocket, and you can imagine the whole fleet lifting off when Pride is over, taking Freddie Mercury and Audre Lorde to the moon. A few blocks east from where I'm writing this is Lake Michigan. I walk there each morning to see where the Belmont Rocks used to be, that cruisey shoreline of sunbaked boulders where Edmund White once pressed his "glossy shoulder" against a lover's "silky thigh." Not far from there is Keith Haring's "Self-Portrait," a sculpture of a planar, genderless figure that stands alone in Chicago's AIDS Garden. In his book *Cruising Utopia*, the theorist José Esteban Muñoz writes about a sublime blowjob Haring gave to the artist John Giorno inside a New York City bathroom sometime in 1982, the same bathroom, perhaps, where White's narrator in *The Beautiful Room Is Empty* went to experience his own "moment of surrender." I don't know what to make of these connecting flights I've been charting through words and bodies and sex. So many of the people who dwelt in these spaces were bound for the pyre, and what remains in their stead is this indescribable sculpture in a stamp-sized garden in Chicago, a garden that was under renovation when I visited, encircled by a chain link fence, off-duty backhoes, this plot of cleared and soured earth.

I'm writing this because I want to pay tribute to the circuits of queer feeling that surge and dwindle in these spaces, because these circuits have wired me, for better or for worse, making me turn on and off in all the ways that I do. I'm writing this because a friend of mine died last December and the last time we said without words that we loved each other was in a gay club in New York that's since gone under, and the last time before that was in another city, another room not long for this world. Rooms came alive when my friend was alive in them. They hummed to a different frequency, a vibe you either get or refuse, so you get it, you hold it down, you move against and beside the body of your friend as, all around you, space is taken and used. I'm writing this, too, because Samuel R. Delany wrote, in 1999, that he was "not interested in the 'freedom' to 'be' 'gay' without any of the existing gay institutions or without other institutions that can take up and fulfill like functions." The pandemic has culled so many of these spaces and might kill off more before it's done. Getting them back will take something more than thirty days slathered with promotional pride. It will take what Berlant and Warner think of as the reinvigoration of "queer counterpublics," what Muñoz heralds as the "concrete possibility of another world," what Delany calls "interclass contact and communication conducted in a mode of good will." Which is to say: all that we have and more.

EDGE

That was the place we'd go when we snuck out of his house at night, to the lake houses just across the road, the dock jutting out into shallows. When the rest of our town was asleep, that metal peninsula was ours. We'd lie there, shivering in our hoodies and gym shorts, the straight-boy drag we still pretended to like, or we'd dangle our feet off the edge of the dock, and by some teenage compact, the mood would turn from jocular to wistful. "Look at that," he'd say, pointing to the far shore, and I'd pretend I knew where he was looking.

On windless nights, the lake below the dock grew so still that the sky seeped down into its mass. Up became down, and down became up. We did not swim on nights like that, for fear we'd break the lake's surface tension. We stayed up on the dock. We watched. The sky still seemed like a long way down from where we were sitting.

I'm writing this in 2022, from Provincetown on the Cape. I've just walked with my partner through the salt- and cum-crusted arcade known colloquially as the "Dick Dock." None of the other gays were down there at such an early hour; they were all up on deck, ordering margaritas. But the sand still held some of last night's footfalls, and there's a feeling of residual surrender—of inhibitions lost and confidences gained—that lingers in a queer space even when it's empty.

Queer phenomenology, Ahmed writes, is an "orientation toward what slips." These days, I'm back at the club till closing time, when the lights come on and utopia sneaks away. The routines I had from before the pandemic have mostly come back. I'm still living with the same man, in the same city. Sometimes, though, I wake up in the morning befuddled; I stare at my bookshelves, and out the bay windows at the children playing tag in the courtyard, unsure of how I managed to make myself a queer berth in this place.

My Kentuckian friend Zach tells me over Zoom he's finally ready to say goodbye to New York, to head back south for a time. "It's like forging a new home in an old place," he says to me. "I'm excited to go back with fresh eyes and a better mindset."

I ask him what he'll miss about being young and gay and gainfully employed in New York City. He mentions the sheer multiplicity of interactions, of choices both sexual and not. He'll miss the diversity of his neighborhood, Washington Heights, how few other cities can provide such a profusion of spaces tailored to queers of all different races and types. But what he'll also miss is that parcel of time he gave up to New York, nearly a decade of zeniths and nadirs, of going out alone as a cure for depression, of cock and menthol and liquor on his breath. He's obviously not alone in having been there and done that, but the city sometimes made him feel that way, and he'll miss that about New York, how gigantically intimate it sometimes could be.

All queers have these spaces we miss, spaces that taught us to be queer, whether or not we lived up to their tutelage. Remember the Carousel before it stopped turning, the cherry stems twisted on ice? Remember the shoreline, the track, the copse beside the highway? Remember what queerness felt like before you even knew its many names? I do. It's an atlas sharing my spine.

The first intentional queer space I ever visited was called "Spectrum Café," a biweekly meetup for LGBT board game enthusiasts held in the basement of a Unitarian church. I went there when I was fifteen with Ellen and Erin, the three of us decked out in lamé leggings and scandalously low-cut vees. I'm pretty sure we knew before we even got there it wouldn't be what we wanted (what we wanted was a bohemian pleasure den, not three elder statesmen who'd brought bean dip and Parcheesi). What keeps me coming back to such spaces is what Muñoz calls "queer potentiality," that state of always being in the antechamber, of having to conjure into being one's place in the world, because that place is never assured. Our expectation, our goal, is not to reach an exalted plane where we and our queer friends can live happily ever after, it's to keep finding novel ways of moving toward the nondescript and often disappointing queer spaces that we have. Following through on these tendencies marks us as those bodies that intend. We are redrawn in these spaces' queer likeness, their slant.

On QTM, the map becomes a mouthpiece for all the spaces we've queered. "Can I call you my home?" asks an intersection in Yogyakarta. "Hi mom, hi dad," squeaks a village in maritime France. Down at the bottom of the map, past even Antarctica, there is a gray zone on the page, a glitch in the grid where a few queer moments have somehow landed. A voice speaks out from this unmappable beltway: "this map is so happysad and I have nothing further to add here."

ROOM (REDUX)

In the beginning, the room is empty, in wait. The door opens. A boy walks in, and then exits when he's ready. What Baldwin wrote is this: "I will not forget the last time he looked at me. The morning light filled the room, reminding me of so many mornings and of the morning I had first come there." Us two in the mirror, an image generated by that space.

In the beginning, the room is built to be left, and I fear it might stay that way forever. But empty space is still heavy with something, and walls stripped of decoration still retain. I hold the room open, bring visitors by for days or weeks at a time. The room moves with me when I move, stays still in my repose: Cambridge, Tucson, Providence, Chengdu. We seldom take breaks from each other, this room and I. We warm up for the friends who drop by unexpected. We make new sentences when we can.

A man eventually takes joint custody of the room, and each year, the lease is renewed. In the room we share right now, one wall is entirely a mirror, and every morning, the mirror's beveled seams diffract the light, dropping rainbows on our duvet. The room is not as lonely as when I entered it, these four walls I've submitted to, this room in which I remember—this room that does my remembering. Neither of us has decided to leave just yet. The water is about to boil, the sofa set up for tomorrow's guests. I tell whoever will listen to stay the course of indecision. I tell them about the room, and how in its most beautiful hours, it's full.

FARRAGUT, 2011

Southings

Southing, *noun*

1: difference in latitude to the south from the last preceding point of reckoning

2: southerly progress

The cicadas began to arrive in the South in May. I suppose *arrive* is the wrong word, as the insects had been in the yard for two years already when my parents bought the property back in 2006, their bodies buried eight or more feet deep in the soil, insect clocks set to a seventeen-year timer. They'd grown older in our unwitting company, outlasting two chickens, four goldfish, three graduating seniors, and at least a couple hundred rabbits. Like billions of their brethren across the country, the cicadas were now emerging in their blackened, red-eyed old age, tymbal subwoofers pumping out this endless, dirge-like song.

"These bugs are seventeen years old," I tell my mother. "The same age as Airik."

"Oh really?" she says, actually impressed. "He's been eating them. I hope they taste good."

Mom is showing me around the backyard as Airik the shepherd-chow mix shuffles along in our wake, a belly full of his contemporaries. Almost two years have passed since last I came south. While I was away, my younger sister graduated and moved north for college, leaving my parents with an empty nest. Dad has gotten into home surveillance. He's acquired a fleet of drones that he uses to take aerial snapshots of the neighborhood. (One went AWOL in a neighbor's tree, and Dad's been too embarrassed to walk over and ask for it back.) Then there's the cheap cameras he's placed around the house, their live footage streamable on his phone. Each night since the pandemic began, Dad's sent the family group text a screen grab from one of his feeds—usually a pixelated image of Airik asleep on the porch—accompanied by the same, repeating message of "Good night and good luck!"

Mom, for her part, has pivoted from child-rearing to plant husbandry. She shows me the vegetable beds out back, each haphazardly planted with Chinese watercress, Chinese chives, Chinese eggplants, tomatoes, strawberries, coriander, a lone bitter melon, some swollen peppers and shriveled string beans. There are white irises in bloom all around us, and a big metal pail filled with dark water and what I think must be lilies.

During the years my siblings and I were growing up here, my parents never seemed to take a shine to the South. They never went on hikes in the Smoky Mountains like they do now, or kayaked in the flooded quarry just south of downtown, or had the time to get involved with neighborhood beautification. And yet, I don't remember them ever complaining about feeling isolated either. "It was very simple,"

Dad tells me. He had a three-point plan when he came here: study hard, get a job, raise a family in America—a plan he has executed up to this point. When I ask him if he ever felt unwelcome in Tennessee, he responds adamantly in the negative. Back then, Japan was America's main economic rival, and in his account, Americans thought of China, not Japan, as their main ally in the East. "I always think immigration is the key thing," he says; letting migrants in should be "compulsory," as long as the immigrants are as diligent as him.

My father became a citizen the moment he was eligible, and when money was no longer a problem, he and my mother acquired green cards for their parents so they could visit us whenever they wished. The long-term goal was always to bring the whole family over, to have my grandparents and uncles and cousins all settle in Tennessee. That never worked out—not least because China is no longer a place that highly educated Chinese people feel they need to leave. Growing up, I always thought that maybe my parents were lonely here in the South, and that maybe if they'd made more of an effort to assimilate, not just in terms of citizenship, but culture, they wouldn't have missed their family so much that they needed their family to come over here.

What friends my parents had when I was young were all drawn from the small and frequently drained pool of local Chinese immigrants—friends who were always decamping for other states or reverse-migrating back to China. My parents sometimes speak of following suit after they retire, of pulling up stakes like the cicadas are doing now, circling back to the dappled treetops where their own, cyclical lives began. A Chinese treatise on war, the one not written by Sun Tzu, describes a maneuver known as "Slough Off the Cicada's Golden Shell," in which a retreating force leaves a copy of itself behind on the battlefield to confuse a gullible opponent. Right now, my parents' backyard is covered in these decoys. They crunch like packing peanuts beneath my feet.

If my parents ever did go back to China, I'd feel like one of the decoys: an amber-colored molt left behind by my predecessors. These shells seem more intact than former selves have any right to be, each with a telltale tear by the head through which their wearers got away. Seeing my parents' yard covered in cicada shells was reason enough to come home this summer: how a skin deprived of its body still stands, clinging crab-like to fence posts and stems. One brisk rain might wash them away, but up until now, they've stayed.

———

One of the few near-universal experiences of being Asian in this country—one that cuts across our many differences of national origin, language, class, citizenship status, and skin color—is the tedious routine of begging the question. This question is asked of us in every imaginable place and situation, so that reporting on its occurrence has even become a cliché of Asian American literature. Whenever I'm asked the question, I often consider just lying and supplying the expected response, dispensing with this whole exercise in which I answer one way—the right way, or the way that seems right to me—thereby forcing my interlocutor to rephrase his question, which he always does, twisting it into a conspiratorial "You know what I mean . . ." or else adding adverbs like *culturally* or *originally* until he procures the desired result. The question is not a racist one in my mind, though it certainly wouldn't surprise me if its askers turned out to be racists. It is a question, ultimately, of geography, and at this geography bee I've made into my life, it is the only question that matters: *Where are you from?*

I was born and raised in the American South, in a suburb of Knoxville called Farragut. For ten of the past fourteen years, I've lived in New England, with the remaining four split between China and Arizona. Yet none of these places have felt like a permanent backdrop to my life in the way that East Tennessee once did. I know this because my mind is often drifting southward even as my body stays sequestered in the North. I'll be riding the subway, looking absent-mindedly down the length of the train car, and suddenly the entire locomotive spyglass will be filled with this verdigris flush, a green that rushes along beneath the city on unseen tracks, reminding me, invariably, of the South. In other words, the trigger is environmental: the way the air is balanced today, the glossy depth of a field my partner and I pass while driving from one Boston suburb to the next, looking for passable dim sum. This field will look, in the brief glimpse of it I can catch, fresh, perfect, unmown.

And so we come to the crux of the matter: a Southern field I once knew. I hesitate to even describe this field, as it really was a prosaic space, a pastoral interlude in the middle of suburbia, as neutral and inviting as only a field can be. Obviously, there was grass in this field; that, and a few trees. I cannot call up specific names for those trees, nor for the many birds, reptiles, and insects that, in addition to me and the cows, must have inhabited that space. Knowing the field in that way never interested me. The field was this outside space, one I did not wish to assimilate into my world, even as I spent hours exploring its expanse. Nowadays, I consider that field—or rather, my attachment to it—as possibly the most Southern thing about me. Although I lack most of the outward tells of Southernness, which is to say I speak unaccented English and have a face that is neither white nor black but yellow, that field *places* me in the South. My memories of it are full-body ones: overgrown, terrestrial, musical as any sentence by my hometown's literary hero James Agee ("Now is the night one blue dew"), lit up like a landscape shot by Sally Mann.

I used to practice wushu out in the field, far away from all my neighbors' prying eyes, stretching and high kicking and making patterns with my limbs. For years, I've had this recurring dream where I'm back there, dressed in my East Tennessee Wushu Team uniform of sky blue polyester, alone and running. It's dawn or early evening, the field's grassy swells covered in fog, and as I run, I start leaping at the crest of each earthen wavelet, and these leaps keep stretching out until I am gliding through air like the warriors in wuxia films do, a body no longer in touch with the ground, predisposed toward flight.

While I'm no expert at dream analysis, the subconscious speaks pretty loudly in this one. I loved that field, but that field belonged to someone else, a farmer who owned the cattle and harvested the hay. Technically speaking, I was a trespasser on this man's property, and so my relationship to *his* field might as well be my relationship to the South as a whole: an enduring fidelity I feel for a space I could never, fully own.

———

IN MAY 2021, DURING A NATIONWIDE SPIKE IN ANTI-ASIAN VIO-lence, President Biden signed off on the COVID-19 Hate Crimes Act, a somewhat nebulous piece of legislation signaling that Congress and the president weren't on board with all these unprovoked attacks on Asian grandmas. Only two months earlier, a white man named Robert Aaron Long had been arrested for a series of lethal shootings at three massage parlors in Georgia (eight people, including six Asian women, were killed in the attacks). Whether or not these killings

SOUTHINGS

counted as a hate crime against Asians, or women, or perhaps Asian women in particular, was still being arbitrated in both the national press and the Georgia courts when I got on a plane and flew to Tennessee. I didn't know right then how I felt about the embattled status of "Asian America." I just knew I wanted to go home.

I've been thinking more than usual about this: the place which Asians do or don't have in that part of America that gets defined as the South. Most of the scholars I've consulted on the topic tell me that "Asian America" and "the South" rarely, if ever, converge, making the Asians at the center of this Venn diagram seem like poor navigators, honorary Californians who somehow wound up in Tennessee. There are many reasons for this incongruence (what the editors of an anthology called *Asian Americans in Dixie* refer to as the Asian Southerner's "discrepant" status). One is simple demographics. Even though Southern cities like Atlanta and Houston boast large and rapidly growing Asian communities, proportionally fewer Asians live in the South than in the West or Northeast. Another factor might be spin. Asian Americans are consistently seen and represented, even by ourselves, as "new" Americans, and the spaces and timelines we populate are reliably contemporary or futuristic. We are proprietary products, that is, of the long twentieth century as well as harbingers of the twenty-first. Our Oort cloud of associations includes "fusion cuisine," "forgotten wars," "globalization," "foreign imports," "software engineer," and "R&D." On the other hand, the South and its people are famously anti-progressive, old and loamy and deeply rooted in all things. Despite all the hubbub about so-called "New Souths," Southern identity is perceived by most to be marooned in the beforetimes, somewhere betwixt Civil War and civil rights. Asians were here in the South back then as well (see the "Manilamen" of the Louisiana bayous, the handful of indentured coolies who labored on Southern plantations, the eight thousand–plus Japanese incarcerated in Arkansas during World War Two), and yet our historical presence in these parts has been easy to forget, our present-day contributions limited to a smattering of Indian-owned motels and Chinese-owned grocers.

As the critic Leslie Bow writes, Asians in the South have long occupied a kind of "social limbo, a segregation from segregation," by which she means that Asians can rarely tell where they fit within the South's racial pecking order. One could, of course, make the same argument about Asians elsewhere in this country. Outside of a few urban enclaves, aren't most Asian communities so small as to barely register within any local patchwork of social relations? Perhaps the aberrancy of Asians in the South is simply a difference in degree, then—we feel more like a minority here than elsewhere, and so more existentially adrift. But the difference also has to do with how the South has itself been framed as a space apart, home to the obese, the poor, and the excessively religious; the bigots and the rednecks; the winsome folk singers and daredevil Davy Crocketts. This vast and heterogeneous region has so often been held up and put down as a different, phantasmal America, and so being Asian in this space means embodying an exception within the exception—an anomaly, squared.

One core tenet of Southern distinctiveness is the intense, almost maudlin connection good Southerners are supposed to feel for the land they were raised on. As a college student in the North, I once attended the office hours of a teaching assistant who'd also grown up in the Tennessee Valley. White Southerners I knew at my school often spoke of feeling out of place there, outclassed by an even older WASP elite. (Some of these Southerners even banded together to form a short-lived "Southern Culture Club," spearheaded by a girl I knew from my freshman dorm who claimed direct descent from Robert E. Lee.) My teacher probably had little interest in discussing Southern identity politics with me, but she also didn't balk when I asked her about her upbringing in East Tennessee. She told me she'd grown up on a farm north of Fountain City with chickens and goats and brothers who shot squirrels, and said that it was only after she, too, left the South for college that she realized hers was not a "normal" American upbringing. Most of the people my teacher knew growing up were only one or two generations removed from agrarian life. This closeness to the land, or at least the land's memory, was what distinguished Southerners from everyone else.

Perhaps this is also why the confluence of Southernness and Asianness has continued to elude me. The former is premised on land: stolen land, broken land, land that has been worked over for generations, but land nonetheless. The latter—if it's built on anything at all—is built on dislocation and diaspora, on the dispersed and fragile networks forged by those who've learned to dwell in spaces few and far between.

This is all to say that there are Asian people in the South—millions of them, in fact—but that doesn't mean they feel Southern.

ON THE SCREEN PORCH IN FARRAGUT, I SIT WITH THE DOG AND the sweltering air. I rock back and forth in the chair as sunlight sews clever little embroideries into a white wooden table. This is the table where I learned how to write—you can still see the imprint of old words, both Chinese and English, grooved onto its surface—and also the table where I once laid a dead king snake after a long walk through the field, its sleek length banded black and white, one of those perfect found objects of summer.

Airik's old, but he's only recently begun to show it. He's acquired a few things since last I saw him: rheumy eyes, occasional fits of flatulence, a custom-built staircase with a railing leading down into the yard (no one with hands ever uses these stairs, but my parents' home insurers insisted on the railing for liability reasons). Petting him as he pants, I pick three or four ticks out of his fur, each like a Botoxed raisin.

Here we are: a man and his dog on the porch, listening to cicadas. Is there any configuration more Southern than that?

Since none of my friends live in town anymore, I spend most of my time at home just driving around, indulging my private nostalgia while playing the part of the Asian tourist. I go to places I never paid much attention to when I lived here, places called Founder's Park, and the Farragut Folklife Museum inside of Town Hall, where one can admire an oil portrait of David Farragut—first admiral of the US Navy, born not far from this spot!—and scope out his wife's collection of fine china. I even go into Knoxville itself, my hometown's recently resurgent core: Gay Street and Market Square, a weather kiosk installed in 1912 that no longer tells the weather. I visit one boring municipal museum, and then another, loiter about a park commemorating James Agee just down the street from my parents' first American apartment. There is a sign by the river welcoming pandemic travelers: "For the Love of Knoxville. Travel Safe. Stay Safe."

I guess this is "the South," or my slice of it at least. My South is that austral shiver I get when I hear Dolly Parton's "The Bridge." It's the mountains blued out by distance that are permanently fixed into a folksy still life in the back of my mind. It's the field: the field as it was, and as it is. When I'm back in this South, I'm always trying to parse where myth and land part ways. At the Museum of Appalachia, I walk around a barn dubbed the Appalachian Hall of Fame, squinting at all the writing on the wall: "These are our people. World renowned, unknown, famous, infamous, interesting, diverse, different. But above all, they are a warm, colorful, and jolly lot. In love with our land, our mountains, our culture." The barn is stuffed with quilts and old photographs, mandolins with frayed strings, the kind of apocrypha (for example, a child's sled owned by the founder of Dunkin' Donuts, who years ago vacationed in East Tennessee) that only such institutions care to retain. Here there is a corner devoted to "Misc & Unusual Indian Artifacts," and beyond that, a bunch of placarded exhibits bearing the colorful stories of Appalachian Hall of Famers, stories like that of Asa Jackson's "Fabulous Perpetual Motion Machine" and "Old 'Saupaw' the Cave Dwelling Hermit and His Little Hanging Cabinet."

None of these stories speak of Appalachian Asians, or of Asians in the broader South. There is no such "representation" to be had at this museum, unless you count, as I do, the kudzu vines conquering all the nearby trees or the Indian peafowl roaming the grounds, pecking away at some invisible prey.

SEVERAL DECADES AGO, ANOTHER ASIAN NAMED CHOONG SOON Kim came to the South in order to study it. Much like my own parents, Kim arrived here as a doctoral student. He wanted to write a treatise on Southern culture, a deep dive into "the 'innards' of the South" as told through the refracting lens of race. The resulting book—*An Asian Anthropologist in the South: Field Experiences with Blacks, Indians, and Whites*—is not so much an objective account of Southern race relations as it is a reflection of how one Asian anthropologist was received in the South.

That reception was not always a warm one. Children followed Kim down the streets of Georgia, chanting, "Chinaman, Chinaman." Multiple informants, mostly educated whites, refused to shake Kim's hand or answer any of his questions, even as they spoke deferentially to his white colleagues. Someone broke into Kim's motel room to steal his field notes and left a threatening note on his car. At one point, a cop bluntly told Kim that no foreigner from an "underdeveloped" country should have the gall to question Americans about their ways. And yet Kim refuses to interpret any of these events as racially motivated, writing in his book's epilogue, "I wish to emphasize that I have never been subjected to [racial discrimination] during my ten years of living in the South."

Confident as Kim might have been that he had never experienced Southern racism firsthand, he nonetheless concludes that Asianness and Southernness are immiscible entities. Unlike the white anthropologist who tries to "go native," Kim realized in the field that it was more expedient for him to play up his foreignness. Southerners were more likely to help him with directions and talk his ear off, slowly, about local happenings if they perceived him as a temporary irritant rather than a potential fellow citizen. Kim's method for getting by in the South was thus to strategically orientalize himself, to "conform to the role of the stereotyped Asian both in my field work and in all other aspects of my life."

It's that "all other aspects of my life" bit that gets me—how someone can learn to flourish in a place without ever integrating into its fabric. Although Kim would spend more than three decades in the South before returning to Korea; although he raised his children here; although he owned property in the South, presumably paid taxes to a Southern state, and taught a generation's worth of Southern students at UT Martin, where he was a professor of sociology until 2001, Kim never came around to seeing himself as a Southerner. It was like his time in the field began the moment he came to the South and didn't finish until he left it: a thirty-six-year study completed by one "nonimmersed Asian ethnographer."

I've been trying to remind myself on this latest Southern journey that my life and project are not the same as Kim's, even if both of us link the South in our minds to a field both abstract and real. He stood outside or above it, his field site, trying to master its conditions. I've long wanted the opposite: to have the field master me.

Perhaps what I'm delineating is just a generational difference. Kim is my parents, or at least the stereotyped version of them I've constructed for easy consumption (terse and hardworking neo-Confucians, unconcerned with social justice and connected always to the old country), while I am their offspring, equally troped: this flighty layabout overfull of misplaced identifications; this second-gen wandering heart desperate to belong.

It seems too direct to ask my parents if they feel like Southerners now, thirty-five years after my father's arrival. The answer, I fear, is liable to be yes and no at once. My mother tells me she never really thought about how Tennessee might be different from anywhere else in America she might have ended up. Her parents were back in China; that was the only geographic distinction that carried any weight. She says she never seriously considered leaving the South, though she does miss the lifestyle she had when living in big cities. "I can visit those places if I want to now," she says. When she retires, she is considering keeping the house here but moving back to China for long stints, staying in hotels and moving around from city to city, like I did years before. She hopes to take her mother with her as she travels, and to bury her father's ashes. My agong passed early in the pandemic, when China was still closed to visitors. Mom and I watched his funeral on WeChat. She has not stopped feeling like a bad daughter ever since.

But being here has also changed her. "I think mostly in English now," she tells me. It took many years for that to happen, but now the sounds in our minds are the same. I ask her if she found it difficult when I was young to communicate with me, a no-brainer kind of question that, right after I ask it, makes us both laugh. "You think it's hard?" she says, turning the question back on me. I lie and tell her I don't remember.

Kim reports meeting someone like me in the course of his fieldwork, a Korean American born in the South named Wilson that Kim chastises as only a disappointed parent can. "He appeared Oriental, but knew nothing about the Orient." And yet this young, oriental man, Southern drawl and all, could also not pass muster as Southern. By the Asian anthropologist's standards, Wilson was a cultural mongrel lacking any "clearcut identity," a con artist who didn't even know he was running a con, this "marginal man belonging nowhere."

———

IT WOULD BE EASY FOR ME TO COMPARE MY OWN ASIAN SOUTH-ernness to bad improv, a mug's game of representations in which what I'm taken for is rarely what I am. Due to the legacy of redlining, my public school and the tony suburb it served were both overwhelmingly white (Black Knoxvillians all lived in North or East Knoxville and attended schools we suburbanites disparaged as "inner city"). So, yes, what Asians there were in Farragut did stick out, and there were times when I thought of us, me and all the Asians I knew, as propertied squatters with no valid claim to this non-Asian place—a place I had the misfortune of loving as much as I did.

Still, it's important for me to note that my own Asian identity did not form inside of a vacuum. My parents were early members of the East Tennessee Chinese Association, founded in 1992, and through that association's various functions, had introduced me to other Chinese immigrants and their kids, some of whom have remained my lifelong friends. The things that bonded me to my fellow Chinese Knoxvillians were not just the strong nuclear forces of race and class and city. It was the baroque specificity of any scene within a scene, all these things I thought no one outside of our tiny East Tennessee/ China enclave could understand, things like our aunts smuggling over seeds from Zhejiang when they traveled; our mothers' late-nineties traffic in VCR tapes, all of Michelle Kwan; or that sigh of relief some of us breathed when it turned out we sucked at violin. It was the lop-sided satellites on our porches that gave our visiting grandparents access to CCTV, and the better-than-passable Sichuan restaurant known as Hong Kong House (RIP), which used to sit like an MSG-laced beachhead by Tennessee's first official state road. It was the miasmic, soul-crushing boredom of Sunday Chinese school weighed against the ethnocentric delights of parties we poopooed to our white friends but secretly relished. It was the magnificent sprawl of those parties, the pool of slip-on shoes at the door, the potluck contributions that deified their casserole containers, the mellifluous blend of Mando-pop karaoke and *Super Smash Bros. Melee.* It was the dads getting trashed at the weiqi table as the moms counted cards in the kitchen. It was learning the rules to all our parents' games, but still sticking to Spades instead.

It was also the fact that one day we'd all leave. Whatever this milieu of ours was, it could not be reconciled with where we were, for where we were was in the South. I remember a night right after graduation when I took all my Asian friends with me to the field. We dragged a bunch of hay bales together into a circle, piled all our homework from AP physics and AP US history and AP calculus in the middle of that circle, and then we set our homework on fire, because there was a lot of it, and the A's we'd made no longer mattered. I don't know what everyone was thinking that night at the bonfire of nerd vanities, but I'm pretty sure it had something to do with how we'd all be gone by summer's end, off to some college north or west of here. This field in the South could not be ours. This field in the South had been caked on in stygian layers, sedimented in stories of decrepitude and succession, in histories always on the edge of forgetting and Southern people laid low by the weight of their benighted land. We would not be those people. We would be fleet of foot, pecunious. We would run until our yellow and brown bodies were lighter than Southern air, air that everyone knows is heavy.

But that's only half the story, the half I've been too eager to tell. In all my years of practicing wushu, the move I most wanted to master was called an "aerial," a cartwheel performed in midair. I always started the move perfectly, my legs tossing up above me, my arms and shoulders relaxed as I somersaulted into flight. Then something in me would falter. My eyes would make contact with the field below. My hand would shoot down to touch it.

JOAN DIDION, A TRUE FOREIGNER TO THESE PARTS, USES THE following phrases to convey what she saw when she came South: "morbid luminescence," "dark like an X-ray," "fever of unknown etiology," "hypnotic liquidity," "precarious emulsion," "decay, overripeness, rotting." Comparing the South to her own home terrain of California,

Didion writes, "In the South they remained convinced that they had bloodied their land with history. In California we did not believe that history could bloody the land, or even touch it."

If Didion is to be believed, then part of Southern identity is not just having a relationship to land, it's having a relationship to land that is mutually toxic. Consider, for example, the Museum of Appalachia's most memorable exhibit: a one-room cabin built by John Clemens, the father of Samuel Clemens, better known as Mark Twain. The elder Clemens built this cabin years before his famous son's birth in Missouri, when the family was based in what is now Fentress County, Tennessee. The cabin made the land inhabitable, and it was that parcel of land that Clemens put his faith in, the land that made him dream. He believed that the mere possession of these Appalachian acres would make his family rich—if not in this lifetime, then surely in the next, when rare minerals spilled forth from every fold of Fentress County: "I shall not live to see those acres turn to silver and gold but my children will. . . . Whatever befalls me, my heirs are secure." Those heirs did end up "secure," but not on account of that land and its losses.

Consider, too, the town of Rocky Top, Tennessee, where I walk past rows of trailer houses, each with at least two NO TRESPASS-ING signs posted. Rocky Top used to be called Lake City before the local council brokered a deal with an investor who wanted to build a water park nearby. The investor promised to sink a hundred million dollars into the project, but only if the residents of Lake City agreed to rename their town "Rocky Top" after Tennessee's official state song. Following a legal skirmish with the estate of the song's writers, Lake City succeeded at renaming itself Rocky Top—as in *Rocky Top, you'll always be / Home sweet home to me*—in 2014. The hundred-million-dollar water park, however, has yet to materialize.

It's the middle of a hot day, and even the children are sheltering in place. The Thursday special at the Vols Diner is catfish, and the antiques store with the native effigy out front just closed. I'm walking past a gas station, feeling light-headed from caffeine, when the thing that always happens starts happening to me. (I don't mean "always happens in the South," as these scenes do not discriminate by region.)

"Hey," says a youngish white man biking on the sidewalk, and I'm already crossing the street, hoping my dodge wasn't too obvious.

"Hey you," he says again. "Do you understand what I'm saying?"

I walk faster, and the man starts to follow me on his bike. "Motherfucker!" he yells now. "Motherfucker! Chink!"

I keep walking and say nothing, though in my head I'm thinking, "Fucking meth head" and "Redneck piece of shit." The man on the bike keeps pace with me.

"Go back to where you came from! Motherfucker! Chink! Motherfucker! Chink!"

"Well, this is fucking stupid," I say to no one but myself, turning off the street and breaking into a run. Without thinking it through, I grab a fist-sized rock off the ground and keep running, wondering if those long-ago years of wushu practice might finally come in handy. But the man soon disappears, the day rectified into silence. There is an empty baseball field in front of me, I notice, and a dead tree drawn and quartered by a chain link fence. I go to my car and just sit there for a few minutes, running the AC. I'm already berating myself for not dealing with the situation in a calmer or more confident way. Why had I immediately crossed the street instead of responding to the man's greeting? Why had I been so quick to pathologize him, that "fucking meth head"? Why had fantasies of violence jumped so readily into my head?

I guess I'm more like Kim than I care to admit. Every time this scene repeats, I try to empathize with the opposition, to rationalize their actions as a neutral observer might, and in so doing, remove their barbs from my skin. I try and do this especially in the South, because in a deeply condescending way, I feel like I owe it to these sad people stuck in sad places, these Rocky Toppers plentiful in pride of place but scarce in everything else. And yet the bitterness in me is also very real, and very Southern. I may be fed up with myself for taking what amounts to schoolyard name-calling so seriously, but I'm even more fed up with them, these men and women who insist on begging the question in the most debasing of ways, these wrathful Southern revenants we honorary whites are supposed to handle with kid gloves or avoid. Why are we not extended, at bare minimum, the benefit of their avoidance? Why is it so hard, when they come calling, to stand where we are and just be?

I'VE BEEN TRYING TO LEAVE THE SOUTH FOR ALMOST FOURTEEN years now. Coming back is partly an obligation, a son visiting his aging parents. But truthfully, I feel out of sorts when I've been absent from the Valley for too long. My little sector of Appalachia is probably the one place on Earth where I can always tell when something has changed. There's now a Kung Fu Tea right next to Tennessee's first highway, and a Pho 99 where a Stefano's Pizza used to be. Near that pho place is Far East, a tiny Chinese grocer where I used to sit on a crackly leather armchair by the door as Mom picked out vegetables, sucking on a gratis Dum-Dum. The kindly source of those Dum-Dums is now dead (lung cancer, Mom says as an aside), and so we do our shopping at a newer and better-stocked grocer called Sunrise. I always stop outside of Sunrise to read the latest notices pinned to the community message board. Today, there are the usual advertisements for badminton lessons, citizenship lawyers, and language exchanges, plus a help wanted sign for Little Caesar's with the tagline JOIN THE EMPIRE printed on it in all caps.

What's also changed, to my sadness and surprise, is the field. Sometime in the last two years, the farmer sold the land and developers swooped in. The neighborhood will be called Ivey Farms when it's finished. People will live there, and not just in their minds. They will lead lives not unlike the one that I led when I was growing up here, which is to say they will need their own outsides.

I must go and see it, obviously, the field before it's no longer itself. It looks rather small, with freshly paved roads circumnavigating its heart. Much of the ground cover has been stripped away to reveal the land's livid, red insides, from which bulwarks of wood, soon to be houses, now rise. I think back to all the hours I spent here as a kid, how the field that wasn't mine still conferred to me a sense of place. I learned my cardinal directions from sitting in that field and adopting its orientation. To the east were always the Smokies, to the west a woodland masking the interstate. My north was a new neighborhood, my south the neighborhood where I still dream. I don't want to leave yet, but there's not much left to see. I consider taking a few tufts of grass with me as a keepsake, but that would be morbid, I think, like shaving hairs off a corpse. As I cut back across the dividing line that separates my parents' neighborhood from the field, I notice I've brought a bit of the field back with me, a few grams of Southern soil, pressed into my soles, that I leave behind me now as tracks.

———

MAYBE THE QUESTION IS ACTUALLY LESS COMPLICATED THAN I've made it out to be. You're either from a place or you aren't; you're

Southern, or something else. I haven't lived in the South since I turned eighteen. Ergo, I'm no longer Southern. What helps me undo this bind is the fact that so much of Southern identity is about missing a place from afar. This is a feeling many Asian Americans are also familiar with, even if the homes they pine for lie further east than Tennessee. To walk around with a vestigial geography in the mind, to feel shackled to a place, whether you want to be or not: these are feelings an Asian Southerner gets from both sides.

This is also how I know that an Asian South does exist. I miss it. It's as simple as that. All the glimmerings of that hybrid strata—the humidity, the cicadas, the scallions bunched up in the yard—and all the habits of mind and body these glimmerings sustain, they're real. My father tells me he wanted to be an artist, too, when he was young— not a writer, but the kind of artist who sketches people in the park. He's very glad he didn't try to go through with that plan, the path of "crazy people," he says. But now that he's older, he's gotten back into picture making, using cameras instead of a pen. "I don't think you could take a picture like this anywhere else," he says of a heavily edited image he's just framed. The picture shows a forest in the Smokies from above, in autumn, the foliage washed in ruby red. Dad has affixed a stamp-style *yinjian*, or signature, to one corner, indicating that this Southern image is his. "Doesn't it look just like a Chinese painting?"

As for my old dog, he coordinates his dying with the cicadas. By July, they're all gone, and I'm reading a pamphlet from the pet crematorium warning me to avoid stewing in this "deafening silence." Mom asks me what I think we should do with the ashes. I tell her we should scatter him in the field before its new tenants move in. When we try and take him out of the urn, though, the lid of the vessel is sealed. "Let's just leave him on the porch then," Mom says. He was sleeping there when he passed.

———

I NO LONGER HAVE THAT DREAM ABOUT FLYING OVER THE field, but that doesn't mean I'm not still dreaming of the South. I like to think that the dream has simply changed: no longer flight, but staying, no longer airtime, but land.

Because the question has been asked and answered, allow me some specificity: I'm from the South. I'm from a part of East Tennessee near where the French Broad meets the Holston. I'm from the town of Farragut, just west of Knoxville. I'm from a neighborhood both like and unlike all the others in my town, and most of all, I'm from a field that no longer exists.

In that field, I'm running with all my friends down summer's gentlest grade. It's past midnight, and in the darkness, I can no longer see where the field ends and the rest of the South begins. We've stripped off our clothes and are streaking as fast as we can through the grass, through dew and through dark. We're not flying yet, we're here, and I'd give up flight forever just to be here again, a disturbance in this field.

Acknowledgments

———

Many people, places, and institutions helped me write this book. My gratitude first to the following:

To the editors of the publications in which excerpts of this book first appeared, often in different form: sections of "The Figure a Trip Makes" in *ANMLY*, "Map Page" in *Entropy*, "Take My Name but Say It Slow" in *Guernica*, "Driving Days" in *New England Review*, "What the River Gave Me" in *New South*, "Phenomenology of a Fall" in the *Offing*, "A Borderlands Transect" in *Quarterly West*, "Love on the Rocks" in the *Southern Review*, and "Running Days" in *Southwest Review*.

To Christopher Combemale for his advocacy and brilliance, Helen Thomaides for her careful and generous edits, Huneeya Siddiqui for gracefully stepping in during the final phase, and the entire team at Norton for helping make this book a reality.

To the teachers who taught me: Darcy Frey, Stephanie Burt, and Naomi Pierce at Harvard; Ander Monson, Chris Cokinos, Fenton Johnson, and Julie Iromuanya at the University of Arizona; Leticia

Alvarado, Ralph Rodriguez, Daniel Kim, and Ada Smailbegović at Brown. I owe a special, heartfelt thanks to Aleeta Johnson at Farragut High School, who first encouraged me to write.

To Lambda Literary, the Sewanee Writers' Conference, and the Virginia Center for the Creative Arts for their dual gifts of community and time. Alex Marzano-Lesnevich and Linda Villarosa offered me advice and encouragement. Min Li Chan presented me with the most remarkable of pinecones. Bernadette Roca helped bring me to the finish line.

To the writers who read and responded to early versions of these essays: Erin Aoyama, Samuel Barber, Francisco Cantú, Sylvia Chan, Abby Dockter, Cherone Duggan, Rafael Gonzalez, Danielle Geller, Lily Hoang, Emily Maloney, Michelle Repke, Zach Shultz, Jae Towle, Katherine Xue, and the members of the Cambridge Asian American Writers' Workshop.

To the friends who spoke to me about their own "queer cartographies": Bryant Brown, Matthew Kateb Goldman, Lauren Krouse, Ally LaForge, Zach Shutz, and Cameron White. And to Emily Strasser, whose book *Half-Life of a Secret* greatly informed my writing about Tennessee, and who kindly answered my questions.

To the friends who traveled with me through so many of these pages: J Antoine, Lynelle Chen, Marley Cogan, Abby Dockter, Hao Feng, Ellen Ford, Julia Hirata, Grant Jones, Lauren Krouse, Andrew Lacasse, Ally LaForge, Thomas Landemaine, Josh Lipson, Meagan Maxon, Erin Or, Michelle Repke, Michael Wang, Bonnie Wong, Daniel Xu. Thank you for always crossing the distance.

To Huimin Luo and Sheng Dai, for giving me every opportunity and more, and to Ashley and David, for supporting me without question. To Mary and Osha, for inviting me into their family.

And to Liam, my love, for building a life with me, and holding me to it.